I LOVE TO TELL

The

Story

100 Stories
from
"100 Huntley Street"

David Mainse

with

Diane Roblin Lee & Karen Stowell

EDITOR: Karen Stowell

RESEARCH: Johanna Webster

COVER DESIGN, PHOTO & CROSSROADS INFO. LAYOUT: Andrew Morrow

BOOK DESIGN & LAYOUT: Diane Roblin Lee, Praise Productions, www.praise.on.ca

FILM by Eclipse Colour

PRINTED by Premier Press, St. Catharines, Ontario, Canada

PUBLISHED IN CANADA by Crossroads Christian Communications Inc.
P.O. Box 5100, Burlington, Ontario, Canada L7R 4M2
Crossroads' website: www.crossroads.ca or e-mail: huntley@crossroads.ca

Scripture quotations, unless otherwise indicated are from the New King James
Version of the Bible, Thomas Nelson Publishers © 1984, 1982, 1980, 1979.

ISBN 0-921702-88-4

Acknowledgements

We wish to thank the following writers for their contributions to this compilation of stories. Their initials follow the individual testimonies they have written.

Diane Roblin Lee   DRL
Ron Mainse   RM
Robert Skinner   RS
Helena Smrcek   HS
Karen Stowell   KS
Gloria Willoughby   GW

Comments by faithful *100 Huntley Street* viewer, Margaret Lindsay, are indicated in script type at the end of many of these stories.

Contents

❧ *Inspiration* ❧

for

I Love To Tell The Story

by David Mainse

Margaret Lindsay's notebooks communicated powerfully to me as I rested last July from quadruple bypass heart surgery. For example, Margaret wrote, "From this moment on, you'll never be alone. God will be your strength in times of trouble. He will be your joy in times of sorrow."

Former World Champion downhill skiier and Canadian Athlete of the Year is Kate Pace Lindsay, daughter-in-law to Margaret and Bud Lindsay of the Ottawa Valley. Kate visited the Lindsays during the time Norma-Jean and I stayed across the lake from their cottage home. She told me about her mother-in-law's notebooks. I asked to borrow those writings and here is the result.

Margaret, while watching *100 Huntley Street* over the past several years had taken notes about the guests and content, and then added her own thoughts about the message that day. About half of the stories of guests from *100 Huntley Street* in this book have Margaret's comments directly from her notebooks. You'll see them in script type at the end of those testimonies.

I cannot begin to tell you adequately how much these stories and Margaret's notes meant in my speedy journey back to health. I knew I must pass on the wealth of these testimonies to thousands more people. There is something here that will inspire everyone. There's a story to fit a family member, a neighbour, or someone who has never opened his or her heart to God. The way to pass on this inspiration is to pass this book around to as many as possible.

Finally, my thanks to Diane Roblin Lee, a free-lance writer, who has frequently been a guest on *100 Huntley Street*. In addition, thanks to Karen Stowell, editor of our *Crossroads Compass* monthly magazine. Diane and Karen took responsibility for most of the stories. Also, my thanks to Norma-Jean, a constant source of encouragement, and to our son Ron, who looked after the publishing details. Thanks to all. This book is proof that *100 Huntley Street* is "Life-Changing Television."

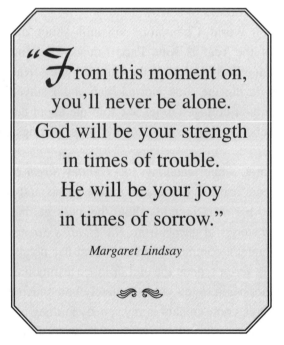

"*From* this moment on, you'll never be alone. God will be your strength in times of trouble. He will be your joy in times of sorrow."

Margaret Lindsay

✌ *1* ✎

Mickey Robinson

Falling to Heaven

"Welcome to *100 Huntley Street!*" As the producer signals directions to the television crew, host David Mainse addresses the camera, warmly welcoming one person – his beloved viewer. With crystal clear blue eyes reflecting the river of life, his passion for souls knows no borders. The viewer, one of the hundreds of thousands watching, is personally engaged with a message of hope.

Waiting in the wings is Mickey Robinson, today's guest, ready to share the story of his personal encounter with God. Through years of television ministry, stories like the one about to enfold have provided a practical school of theology, unmatched by the prestigious corridors of academia – extraordinary evidence of God's reality through the lives of ordinary people.

In 1968, Mickey Robinson was a 19-year-old with an insatiable thirst for adventure. Raised in a dysfunctional family, his traditional religious schooling did little to awaken any interest in spiritual things. While he knew all about God, no one had ever told Mickey that he could have a personal relationship with Jesus. Anyway, as far as he was concerned, he could handle anything that came along himself. Little did he know that life can change forever in one instant of time.

Fascinated by anything to do with the sky from earliest memories, he signed up for flying lessons, but soon discovered that what he really wanted to do was jump out of the planes! Free-falling became his passion. The only problem was that the "high" lasted for only about 66 seconds, leaving him with the same old gnawing hunger for lasting fulfillment. Vaguely, he thought that if he could just get more adventure, be successful in his stockbroker career and get the right girlfriend, he'd fill up the emptiness inside. During a routine parachute jump, those ideas changed.

At an altitude of 13,500 feet, the Piper Cherokee's engine quit and had an aerodynamic stall. Falling out of the sky like a dead duck, the plane crashed into a huge oak tree at 100 m.p.h., cartwheeled on its wings and burst into flames with Mickey and the pilot trapped inside. One of the skydivers who had jumped just prior to the stall made his way to the plane and, with super-human strength and bravery, extricated Mickey.

Soaked with gasoline and on fire from head to toe, he had sustained brain injury and third-degree burns to 35 percent of his body. With mind-bending pain, crippling nerve damage to his paralyzed legs, his face torn totally open, bones sticking through his flesh and the onset of deadly infections, the doctors gave no hope of survival. As his body began shutting down, the family held a vigil.

Suddenly, Mickey felt himself being ejected from his body into the realm of the spirit. On the instant he left his body, he knew that he had entered the real world. Shocked to realize that the real Mickey was a spiritual entity (the spirit of a person does not die when the physical body does), he found himself travelling towards a beautiful white light. On either side he could see a dense blackness, so thick he could almost taste it, threatening to engulf him. It was void, eternal and non-negotiable – more horrible and hopeless than anything imaginable.

Horrified at the understanding of what it would be like to be cut off for eternity, Mickey began to scream a prayer: "God, I'm sorry! Give me another chance! I want to live!" Suddenly, it was as though the white light was eclipsed and he was standing in heaven in the presence of the Almighty. There he experienced the glory of God like liquid gold radiating all around and through

him – His power and His authority and all of His eternal promises – washing away every tear. Mickey knew that he would
never die. "It's the most alive feeling that you can imagine
because He is the very essence of life."

Then God began to show Mickey future horrors of the world
as though on a big-screen TV, dramatized by close-up views of
faces he had never before seen – and then He showed him that
He was going to send him back. "No," Mickey protested, "I
don't want to leave!" Once again, his spirit travelled through
space and time, then merged with his body. As he looked up at
the ceiling, his mouth opened and he heard the most beautiful
sounds expressing praise to God in a language he had never
learned.

Eventually, following about 75 operations and five years in
and out of the hospital, God
instantaneously restored
Mickey, totally healing his
paralyzed legs and withered
feet. According to one of the
doctors, it couldn't be called
a healing because in many
aspects, there was nothing to
heal – it was a creative
miracle. Now, amazingly,
Mickey is skiing with his
kids again – and occasionally skydiving! But there is no
"high" that compares with
knowing God.

Now Mickey knows
why he's here. He's a messenger of hope for those who
have none. —DRL

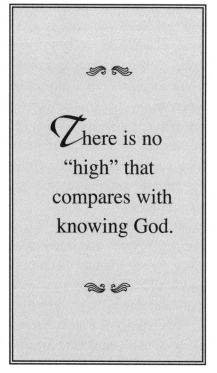

There is no
"high" that
compares with
knowing God.

❧ 2 ❧

Frank & Irene Camisso

A Family Reached For Christ!

If you're ever visiting the church where the Camissos worship, you'll recognize Papa Frank, adored patriarch of the Camisso clan. He's the broad-shouldered man sitting on the far side with his lovely blonde wife surrounded by their three daughters, two of their three sons-in-law and all nine grandchildren. The other son-in-law, John Blair, is the "larger-than-life" blonde fellow either on the piano, drums or guitar. There's a good chance it will be his turn to lead praise and worship the day you're there. If you make it out to a church dinner, you'll find the whole clan waiting on tables, cooking in the kitchen or doing the dishes. If there's a way to wangle an invitation to their home, you won't forget the visit. No matter who you are, they'll be genuinely happy that you honoured them with a visit.

While it may appear that Frank and Irene have been pillars of the church forever, they haven't. Although introduced to the Lord back in the '50s at a Billy Graham Crusade, weekends at the cottage contributed to a gradual drifting away from their commitment.

It was just in the mid-'80s that a niece told Irene about *100 Huntley Street*. "And it has changed my family!" she exclaims. "Now we are a family that loves the Lord – and this includes our grandchildren. He promises to give us life and to give it to us more abundantly."

According to Frank, the Lord's hand was upon them all along: "I don't think God forgets that initial commitment. I don't think we are ever out of His sight!" Having found God's promises remained true, even through times of very deep waters like that of Irene's battle with cancer, Frank has developed full confidence in God's ability to provide leadership to his family.

Over a period of time, Frank and Irene's three daughters – Susan, Alice and Barbara – also began watching *100 Huntley Street*. Since then, each of them, along with their husbands and children, have given their lives to Christ! He has worked very differently, yet powerfully, in each of the three families.

When Susan, the eldest, and her husband, John Blair, were confronted with the sudden loss of their adopted daughter Katie at the age of two due to a fatal genetic disorder, only the supernatural peace and comfort of God gave them the strength to carry on. Susan says, "At that point, I thought my world was over, and wondered how I could go on after losing a treasure like Katie, so I called out to the Great Comforter and He was there."

When John arrived home to the horror of Katie's unexpected death, he immediately sensed God's presence in the room. "God's Word says that He is the Comforter, and that He blesses and comforts those who mourn. I understand what that means now, and I thank Him for this promise every day."

> "*I* don't think we are ever out of His sight!"
>
> *Frank Camisso*
>
> ❧ ❧

Alice and her husband, Scott Burns, agree. "We are so grateful to *100 Huntley Street* for being that bridge to Jesus for our family," Alice says. "Prior to my salvation, I felt very much like many people do today – that because I'm a good person, I'll go to heaven. While watching *100 Huntley Street*, I saw there was something more and I was missing it."

As Alice began to focus on her Saviour, Scott noticed a change in her priorities. "Through Alice's salvation and prayers, I kept taking steps closer and closer. In August of '85, I felt humbled before God and gave my heart to Him, and I'm thankful that our four boys have as well."

Although Frank and Irene's high-spirited third daughter, Barbara, always had an awareness of God in her life, she had never felt the need to go to church. However, like the other members of her family, she began to watch *100 Huntley Street*. Fascinated by the testimonies, she soon became aware of her need for Christ. "*100 Huntley Street* is what really led me to my belief in the Lord and to a church," she acknowledges.

Even though Barbara's husband, Paul Baxter, was the son of a minister, he went through a period of rebellion. "As some of us preacher's kids do, we tend to rebel at times," he admits. "After spending many years rejecting my Saviour in the back pew of church, I accepted Christ. In fact, it was through a friend of Crossroads – the late Ernie Hollands. I'm very thankful for that and also for the Crossroads Ministry."

> "*We are so grateful to 100 Huntley Street for being that bridge to Jesus for our family.*"
>
> *Alice Burns*

Today, Frank and Irene have the assurance of knowing that their family will all be together in heaven with the Lord and their granddaughter Katie. Irene adds, "There will be no more good-byes in heaven and that is something we are grateful for." —DRL & KS

❧ 3 ❧
Ron Pearce

The Book of Acts – Fresh!

Millions of young people are raised in Christian homes in North America, as was Ron Pearce. Sadly, the majority of those who remain in the church grow up to be lukewarm Christians – overfed babies, so stuffed with the surfeit of material things that they are dulled to any understanding of repentance, sacrifice or the true power of God. To them, seeking God's will for their lives means figuring out a way to get the most impressive car possible; to drive to the most lucrative job they can find; to pay for the biggest house they can finance; to house selfish children in their own "Christian homes." Occasionally, they whine about the lack of miracles in the church but quickly turn their attention back to sports, sitcoms or soaps.

Once in awhile, someone looks up – as did Ron Pearce.

Ron accepted Jesus into his heart at the age of 13. In his second year of Bible college in Regina, Saskatchewan, he became frustrated with the traditional church. What he experienced there had no resemblance to the activities of the believers described in the *Book of Acts*. As he feasted on the essence of Christianity within those pages, he began to crave the reality and power which was obviously so normal to the early church. For a whole year, Ron desperately sought to be "endued with power from on high." After seeking with all of his heart, he truly found God and was baptized in the Holy Spirit in 1972. From that moment, his life and ministry were radically altered and his personality was transformed.

With an eye on the global picture, Ron and his wife Nancy trained as missionaries. He became the Canadian Vice President of

Bibles International (now WorldServe Ministries). This led to extensive travel throughout the world, visiting such areas as Europe, Russia, Brazil, Cuba, Vietnam, India, China and Hong Kong. With firsthand accounts of the remarkable things God is doing in countries all over the world, Ron speaks to churches, groups and individuals, sharing the fires of revival that burn in the hearts of people throughout the earth.

Listening to Ron, there is no distraction in terms of admiration for the man. While there is much to be admired about him in the natural sense, he is so focussed on the marvellous stories of the love of God throughout the world, that he draws no attention to himself. Thus, with tears and humour, wherever he can find it, he is able to carry the listener with him to witness the 17-year-old pastor in India (a Christian for just six months) powerfully drawing throngs of people to know Jesus as their Saviour; the 16-year-old girl beaten for her faith and now recovering in Nepal; the church in Siberia inflamed with the Spirit of God; the wonder of 84 million precious Christian brothers and sisters in home churches in China; the recently imprisoned Chinese pastor reciting, *"Greater is He who is in me, than he who is in the world."*

Seeing clips of film footage, like that of the Russian General singing the Lord's Prayer with the Red Army Choir, flies in the face of the kind of news clips usually seen at 6 p.m. Looking at a sample of the new handbook for the Russian Army, a New Testament in khaki green with *Steps to Peace with God* by Billy Graham in the back of each, defies emotional description.

Along with positive stories of tremendous spiritual developments around the world, Ron pinpoints areas of great need. While God is pouring out His Spirit in Vietnam, it remains a hot spot – needy for prayer and support. While the Cuban people are hungry for God and coming to Christ, there is great oppression there.

Ron's stories are so thrilling that the listeners, many stirred from their apathy for the first time in a long while, are inspired to reach out from where they are to share in the work of WorldServe Ministries. Others, in whom the fire of Christ burns brightly but are unable to travel as Ron does, are challenged with an opportunity to become involved in missions.

With his international focus, however, Ron remains a Canadian. He weeps for his country of birth when he meets missionaries from oppressed lands sent here to share the Gospel of Christ. He knows that materialism reigns on the throne of North America, and until we respond to the Spirit of God in repentance, there can be no revival. —DRL

In Canada, houses, cars, boats and materialism, in general, mean more than Christ. We need repentance and revival. Come and be filled with the Holy Spirit. We need a hunger and passion for Jesus.

❧ 4 ❧
Janice Humphreys

From The Darkness of Tragedy... To Light and Hope!

It was after midnight when the doorbell rang. The date, Janice Humphreys will never forget – August 24, 1977 – for her life would never be the same again.

A police officer stood at the door, looking apprehensive. Nervously he asked, "Do you have a daughter named Lori?" When she affirmed that she did, he explained that there had been an accident and that Lori was dead. She was only 16 years old.

This was the beginning of a long and painful journey for the family as they sought to come to terms with the loss of a beloved daughter and sister. One might think that such an experience would automatically draw the family together. But this was not the case, as each one walked their own path of grief.

Janice recalls, "When Lori died, it seemed that my ability to love died with her. I did the necessary care-giving, but I was dead on the inside. This is very destructive to both a marriage and to the surviving children."

One evening six months later, Janice was seated at the television not really watching when she heard the words on a Christian program, "Have you ever asked Jesus to take over your life, to be your Saviour and Lord?" Janice realized that although she did attend church, she had never actually accepted Jesus as her own Saviour and Friend.

Janice continues, "As I surrendered my life to Christ, a warmth enfolded me and a bubbly feeling began in my chest and rose to my throat. I was filled with such joy, I just wanted to shout, 'Hallelujah!'"

The next day her neighbour exclaimed, "What happened to you – your eyes are so alive?" Janice suddenly realized the terrible heavy pain in her chest was gone. The Lord had begun to lead her along the path of healing. Through His help, she was able to provide the love and comfort needed for her husband and children. Since then, many members of her family, both immediate and extended, have also committed their lives to the Lord.

Janice became an avid viewer of the daily *100 Huntley Street* program where she learned to know the Lord in a personal way and gained strength to cope with her bereavement.

Janice concludes, "When someone precious dies, there is a need to keep their memory alive. Nothing appealed to us until we heard about the Crossroads Walk of Faith. The concept seems so appropriate to us that we have committed to a memorial stone in Lori's memory. It seems so right that out of our darkness something can be done to bring light and hope to others." —RS

～ 5 ～
Dr. Maurice Rawlings

Heaven or Hell?

Give me a good honest agnostic anytime over an atheist. I can respect an agnostic. He or she makes no claims, simply saying, "I don't know if there's a God," with a shrug of the shoulders and a mind open to discovery.

An atheist, on the other hand, is among the most arrogant of individuals on the planet. By categorically stating, "There is no God," he or she implies having personally studied all of the knowledge of the universe – past, present and future – and confirmed that God does not exist. Who can respect that? People claiming to be atheists are a dime a dozen as long as they're healthy and successful; but when they die, according to Dr. Rawlings' research, they have to change their theology.

Dr. Maurice Rawlings, for many years a specialist in internal medicine and cardiovascular diseases at the Diagnostic Centre in Chattanooga, Tennessee, didn't think much about God. Although he had gone to Sunday school as a child and learned about salvation, he had stuffed all those old prayers and what he considered "hocus-pocus" into a dusty file in the back of his mind labelled, "Irrelevant Info." His career was his life.

One day, Charles McKaig, a patient who had experienced chest pains, showed up in his office. In the process of diagnosis, Dr. Rawlings had him step on the treadmill for an EKG. Within seconds, the man, as he later explained, collapsed and saw the fiery entrance to something like the opening of a volcano before him. In the flames, he could see faces of people in torment, but they were not being consumed by the inferno.

Aware only of the convulsions and clinical death of his patient, Dr. Rawlings performed resuscitation, whereupon, Mr. McKaig screamed, "I've been to hell – I need help!" After this had happened several times, Dr. Rawlings, scrambling to keep the patient calm while he frantically worked to save him, reached back in the dusty file marked "Irrelevant Info." and pulled out a prayer he'd heard years before. Instructing Mr. McKaig to repeat it the next time he got him breathing, he was shocked to discover that after the man died and came back again this time, he was totally peaceful, claiming to have experienced the protection of God as he travelled towards a beautiful bright light.

That day, a double conversion took place in Dr. Rawlings' office. There could no longer be any doubt in the mind of either man that God and Satan – and heaven and hell – were realities.

Having had the filing cabinet of his mind thrown into illogical disarray, Dr. Rawlings was curious. Was this an isolated incident? Does man have a spirit that leaves the body and goes somewhere at the point of clinical death? Does death represent the end of this life or the beginning of another? Is it possible to know what happens after death? Is there evidence to support the Biblical descriptions of heaven and hell? Why, until now, had he heard only of "heaven experiences"?

Determined to find answers, he began to pay careful attention to those he resuscitated. Focussing on "flat-liners" medically retrieved from actual clinical death, he questioned them immediately upon their return to life and documented their descriptions of what they experienced after periods of absent heartbeat, absent breathing and absent vital functions. In almost every case, the patients reported a full sequence of analytical events... many of them occurring in very unpleasant environments.

Among Dr. Rawlings' findings was the fact that descriptions of "hell experiences" are usually heard only immediately following a return to life. The experience is so traumatic that the mind will block the memory or the patient will be too embarrassed to reveal that he or she went there. Christians invariably describe wonderful "heaven experiences."

Dr. Rawlings compiled his findings into his first book, *Beyond Death's Door*. It was followed by *To Hell and Back*. A compelling video by the same title featuring interviews with many of the patients documented in the book, can be downloaded free of charge at: members.truepath.com/freevideo/

Following a life-after-death experience, people report profound effects on their understanding of personal life purposes and beliefs – and there's not an atheist in the bunch. —DRL

⚈ 6 ⚈

Jessica Johnstone

Modern-Day Mary Magdalene Finds Christ

In a fast-paced society where pressures and deadlines are considered a normal way of life, living in the country may seem an ideal alternative. But for newly-married Jessica Johnstone, the transition of moving from a busy city to the stillness of a small rural community was difficult. It meant adjusting to the fact that suddenly her family and friends were a thousand miles away.

Along with feelings of isolation and loneliness, Jessica felt ashamed when she reflected on her troubled teen years in the city. Having experienced a painful childhood, she had ventured out on her own at the age of 15. "By the time I was 16," she adds, "I was an alcoholic. By the time I was 17, I was a drug abuser and had begun to beg, borrow and steal for cocaine."

One thing led to another and soon Jessica's young life was out of control. The addiction, bondage and confusion led her further down the pathway of destruction. When photographed for pornographic pictures at the age of 18, a sense of revulsion and shame had engulfed her, even though she was never taught what

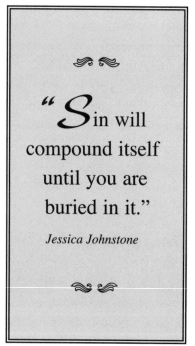

> "*S*in will compound itself until you are buried in it."
>
> *Jessica Johnstone*

was "right" or "wrong" in terms of Biblical values. With hindsight and Godly wisdom today, she explains, "Sin will compound itself until you are buried in it... but the Lord had His hand on my life."

Moving to Alberta proved to be a blessing after all. In the midst of her loneliness and search for real meaning, Jessica began watching *100 Huntley Street*, which she says gave her a sense of being with "family." When David Mainse invited viewers to pray the sinner's prayer, Jessica thought to herself, This is right; this is true. "I then knelt down and prayed along with David," she adds. "There were no lightening bolts or flashes, but there was a peace.... I could really sense God's love and forgiveness."

The change in Jessica's life over the years has been dramatic: "I have gone from a Mary Magdalene to what I am now." Today Jessica joyfully serves the Lord by ministering to others through music and reaching out to her community with His compassion. She concludes with a timely challenge for God's people: "We are living in exciting times! Yet we all need to be prepared to help others who will be giving their hearts to the Lord." —KS

≈ 7 ≈

Louise Fulton

Knowing God as Husband to the Widow

With her tears reflecting the mellow glow of Christmas lights, Louise Fulton sat alone beside the carefully trimmed tree. Her 17-year-old twin daughters, Amy and Jewel, had finally settled into their beds, but still slept fitfully, having so recently watched their father's coffin being lowered into the ground.

It was less than a month since Louise's husband, Gerry, had finally succumbed to a nine-year illness and died. Despite the fact she had known that he would not live, she was still numb from the shock of his death.

What now? she wondered. The preceding years, while filled with Gerry's care and its associated worries, had at least been filled with his presence. Now he was gone and this new emptiness was painfully unfamiliar. Louise went over to the stereo, put on a favourite praise and worship tape, and sat back in her chair. She closed her eyes and allowed the melody to draw the pain out of her aching heart. Like healing oil, the words penetrated her memory, refreshing Scriptures that she had learned as a child.

She remembered the years when she, too, had sung as part of a praise and worship team. Music had been part of her life even as a child, when she and her sisters sang as a trio. One of the things so special to her about Gerry had been his voice and the opportunities they had been given to sing together.

As the praise music continued, Louise's mind went back to the time when she almost died from swallowing pills at five years of age. Although doctors were initially unable to find a heartbeat, Louise had survived. God had obviously had a plan for her life. Just as He had preserved her at that time, He had allowed the loss of Gerry in her life now. God's plans for her had not changed, despite the fact that she saw one circumstance as a blessing and the other as a loss.

> *G*od had a plan for her life... and His plan had not changed, despite the fact that she saw one circumstance as a blessing and the other as a loss.

Louise remembered the Scriptures where God promised that He would be a husband to the widow and a father to the fatherless. For one needing the comfort and companionship of a husband, those words were like the purest gold. Equal to her need for a husband, was the need of a father for her teenage daughters.

In the years since that time, Louise has found God to be true to His Word. He has indeed provided her with love, companionship, leadership and every kind of provision for her life. Her daughters have not been left alone, but have been given the Comforter, in the Person of the Holy Spirit.

With the depth of understanding and compassion that her experiences have given to her, Louise became a great asset in her work as executive assistant at the Open Door Christian Drop-In Centre. There she gave the comfort wherewith she had been comforted. —DRL

∂ *8* ≈

Todd Bender

Investing in Lives

The children's faces beam with delight as they quickly motion the actions of a song that speaks of Jesus' love. For a good number of these inner city kids, it is the love of God that has broken down the barriers of poverty, abusive backgrounds, racial differences and isolation.

Despite the fact that hundreds of children have packed the auditorium, it is evident by the enthusiasm of children's evangelist Todd Bender and his ministry team that each one of these youngsters is so very special.

"Time is of such essence to us," Todd explains. "We want every single child to have the opportunity of personally knowing Jesus. We take the 'last days' mentality that every second counts, for there may only be one chance to reach that child."

Todd knows from his own childhood experiences, the importance of building spiritual values into a child's life. He states, "My grandfather was a German Mennonite, so that kind of flowed over into my upbringing."

The only other means Todd had of learning about the things of God was during his summers at Circle Square Ranch. In fact, it was there he responded to the simple salvation message. "As a child, I thought I understood the whole concept of God (when you die you go to heaven), but I wasn't taught that I needed to confess my sins and receive salvation."

When Todd returned to his rural home, there was no church nearby for him to attend. However, the ministry of Circle Square Ranch sent him letters of encouragement. "It's an amazing thing for a child to receive letters in the mail, especially when living in the country where one almost never gets mail!" he adds.

Throughout his childhood, God's hand remained on Todd's life. "No matter where I was – even when I was hanging around with my unsaved friends who were smoking and drinking – I always had a consciousness about God being with me."

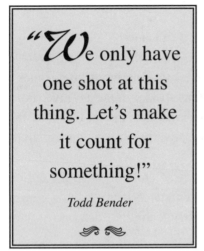

"We only have one shot at this thing. Let's make it count for something!"

Todd Bender

The reality of God's abiding presence became even more real as the teen years progressed. And during this time, his connection to the ranch continued. "They were very significant times in my life," He states. "In fact, Circle Square Ranch was a very big part of our family. My older brother David ended up becoming a ranch program director, and I became a counsellor."

This proved to be a valuable experience for Todd, who was destined to work in full-time ministry with children and teens. Today he heads up a team of six staff and over 60 active volunteers, providing bus transportation for an average of 350 inner city children each week for Saturday Sunday school.

The Generation Now City "Kidz" ministry team also personally visits the homes of about 700 children and teens each week – including their families – encouraging them to attend neighbouring churches on Sundays.

Todd concludes, "When we invest in a person's life, we have no idea the magnitude it's going to have. When one person is saved, he or she will touch two, then they'll touch two, and who knows just where it transcends from there.... We only have one shot at this thing. Let's make it count for something!" —KS

➳ 9 ➳

$\mathcal{P}aul$ & $\mathcal{M}arg$ $\mathcal{R}obertson$

Knowing God in Times of Crisis

Despite the fact that Marg Robertson had loved going to church and singing in choirs throughout her childhood, she had never personalized the message of Jesus Christ.

As a respected school teacher, she considered herself a good person with no major problems in her life and no need of anything beyond what she had. With a great, great-uncle having served as a medical missionary in India many years before, there was a certain sense of membership in an exclusive club of acceptability. God had always been important to her, but until she heard and understood the Gospel message on *100 Huntley Street*, Christianity was more a social than a personal experience.

"God-incidentally," at the same time that Marg discovered *100 Huntley Street,* her mother, who had been a Christian for many years, began to watch *The 700 Club*. She eagerly read the books they recommended and passed them on to her daughter. As the contents of the books were made alive by the power of the Holy Spirit, the ensuing discussions became lively. Mother and daughter were discovering life with a deeper understanding of the Holy Spirit and would never again be the same. As the hosts explained how to invite Jesus into their hearts and lives, Marg also accepted Him.

Meanwhile, Marg's husband Paul was watching his wife. The changes he began to see convinced him that something real was happening. He began to go to church with Marg and he, too, accepted Christ.

Paul Robertson is now in full-time ministry and well known in the Christian community as the Director of Church and Family Resources for Youth for Christ. Marg believes that her primary ministry is to support her husband, raise responsible, well-adjusted children, and minister to the children she teaches in the public school system.

In 1988, the Robertsons were catapulted into every parent's nightmare, when their 11-year-old son was hit by a car. With close friends having lost their son just two years earlier, the depths of what potentially faced them was still fresh.

Utterly distraught, Marg rushed to the hospital. When first approached by the cleaning woman in the emergency ward, she had no idea what would follow. The woman spoke to her with a calm assurance, claiming the Lord had told her that the boy would be alright. When she quoted Scripture, the words resonated in Marg's heart and she knew that the woman was speaking directly from the Lord.

In one brief moment in time, everything that was important in life came into focus for Marg. God showed her that even if everything around her appeared out of control, He was there – in control. Everything rested in His hands.

Thankfully, plastic surgery for scar tissue in their son's forehead was successful, but even more important was his ability to forgive the driver of the car and his subsequent spiritual growth.

The years since Paul went into full-time ministry have been years of adjustment for the entire family. With unique frustrations and rewards inherent in the work, unique approaches to resolving difficulties and receiving blessings have to be found.

Marg and Paul have discovered that Scripture is not just a practical manual for everyday living, but also a guide for effective ministry, a marriage manual, and a solid resource for crisis management. —DRL

✍ *10* ✍

Susan Hofmeister

The Greatest Gift

The scene of the three children around the decorated Christmas tree appeared almost picture perfect. As Susan Hofmeister watched her "cherubs" busily investigating their colourfully-wrapped gifts, her mind went back to past years when they spent each Christmas as one big happy family.

Suddenly, it was as if a cold draft swept through the room, awakening Susan to the reality of her shattered dreams. To add to the pain of her marriage breakup, was the uncertainty she faced upon hearing the doctor's verdict. "The week before that Christmas of '95, I was diagnosed with cancer," she states.

In the midst of all the massive confusion and disarray in her life at that time, Susan became even more desperate in her plea for God's help and a greater understanding of spiritual truth. Surprisingly, He answered in a way she didn't expect: "Shortly after looking up into the heavens and saying, 'God help me!' I stumbled across *100 Huntley Street*. I'm not a TV person, but I was really searching to find out who God was in comparison to the man-made rules I had been taught as a child."

In response to her heart's cry, the Lord began to use the means of Life-Changing Television to reveal to Susan her need of salvation. "*100 Huntley Street* was literally my saving grace. That's where I was getting my spiritual food and my guidance. That was the leadership that was feeding me and guiding me."

Soon after receiving a letter from the Crossroads Ministry Centre referring her to a church in the area, Susan began attending Sunday mornings regularly with the children. "The rest is history," she says. "I've become involved with the youth, and I teach a Sunday school class. It's such a wonderful church!"

Since then, her husband has also committed his life to the Lord and began attending services every Sunday with the family. He has even participated with Susan in a midweek marriage ministries program in order to strengthen their marriage after a one-year separation. "I am learning all that God intends a man to be in relation to his family," he adds.

Susan is in awe of all God's blessings in their lives: "Since undergoing surgery, I'm now free and clear of cancer, and enjoying good health. The Lord has also worked on our marriage relationship. After all, He is in the healing business, and He restores families and heals broken hearts. We now tell our children that the greatest gift we can give them is the opportunity of knowing Jesus. They thank Him for bringing His peace and joy into our home." —KS

∽ *11* ≈

Dr. Orville & Dorothy Messenger

A Surgeon's Life with AIDS

Dr. Orville Messenger was a well-known thoracic surgeon and former chief surgeon in a large Canadian hospital. At the age of 42, with a brilliant career before him, Dr. Messenger was diagnosed with a serious heart condition which required immediate surgery. During the procedure, a blood transfusion was found necessary. Following his successful operation and recovery, Dr. Messenger was released from the hospital.

Eight months later, after routine follow-up testing, the devastating news came that he had received AIDS contaminated blood. The death knell was sounded just before Christmas that year when it was determined that he was HIV positive. With four children and his life's work to consider, Orville and Dorothy made the decision to tell no one of their plight. With the public reaction to the disease still being sensationalized, they felt that privacy was the only way to protect their children from the stigma of AIDS.

Thus began the loneliness of the ensuing ten years before Dr. Messenger's body succumbed to the ravages of the disease in 1995. Because of the wall of secrecy that separated him from outside relationships, despair, thoughts of suicide and the cold reality of isolation from all that was normal dogged him daily. Society's lack of understanding of the disease made it clear that he could not even turn to his church for support. He felt shunned.

Through it all, Dorothy helped Orville to see the situation within the context of God's perfect will. Gradually, he became aware of an astounding sense of the constant presence of God. Because of the resulting peace, the two decided to trust Him in the difficult decisions with which they were faced. Despite the fact that it didn't always seem to make sense according to the established practices, they were faithful to their choice to follow God's direction.

What was expected to be a short period of time before the onset of serious symptoms, turned into a nine-year "autumn." Sadly, its pleasures were always obscured by the thoughts of what would follow, from which there was no expected recovery. During the nine years, Orville and Dorothy began a family diary, journalling their efforts to survive with AIDS. What emerged was a story of social isolation, and a struggle to maintain privacy and reasonable family normalcy in a climate of public fear and ignorance about HIV. In the process of detailing the journey to combat depression, the realization surfaced that the material could be helpful to others in providing a better understanding and means of coping with the disease of AIDS.

Borrowed Time – A Surgeon's Struggle with Transfusion-Induced AIDS is the book that was given birth through Dorothy and Orville's journal. It is rich with evidence that even in the midst of personal disaster, support can be found from the challenges of a new career, special friends and faith in Jesus Christ. —DRL

It's important to offer knowledge to others (Psalm 94:19).

∽ 12 ∾

Jack & Martha Hiebert

God Turns Sorrow Into Joy!

Each Christmas season typically brings with it a sense of anticipation and excitement. Thoughts of gathering together with family and friends for this annual holiday event have most households busily making preparations well in advance. But for those who have experienced loss – whether through death or family break-up – what is supposed to be one of the most joyful times of the year can be the most difficult.

Such was the case for Jack and Martha Hiebert, whose own family was affected by divorce. However, Jack and Martha didn't give up hope. Instead, they put their trust in God to work all things together for good (Romans 8:28). As partners of the

Crossroads Family of Ministries, they understood the importance of prayer. Tucked into an envelope with their donation was a prayer request for the salvation of their loved ones. And God answered....

The first set of miracles took place in 1995. As part of their typical daily routine, Jack and Martha tuned their TV remote to *100 Huntley Street*. To their surprise, there was a special children's segment on that week. Jack was so impressed by the program that he decided to videotape the rest of it for their three granddaughters. And sure enough, when the girls came over for a visit, they thoroughly enjoyed the lovable characters, sing-along action songs, and adventurous stories – all of which helped implant the message of the Gospel into the hearts of these precious young lives.

Near the close of the program, David Mainse asked the children in the studio audience if they had anything they would like to say. One little girl by the name of Melanie sweetly responded, "I want to ask Jesus into my heart." Immediately, David seized the opportunity to invite all the children and families watching *100 Huntley Street* in homes across the country to join him in a prayer of salvation. Upon hearing this, each of Jack and Martha's granddaughters – Ashley, Brooke and Kayla – asked Jesus to come into their hearts too!

Although elated over the girls' salvation, these wise grandparents knew that this was only the beginning of what God wanted to do. Their granddaughters' spiritual growth was then added to the prayer list. "They needed a lot of prayer support that the Lord would encamp around them," Jack points out. "Only then would these little plants be able to stand and grow."

More prayer was lifted up before the Lord on behalf of their concerns, and again He faithfully intervened. "Even if we think it should have worked out differently, God has made something beautiful out of the situation," Martha states. "In the summer of

'97, our son's girlfriend Guia became a Christian through some girls that she worked with."

Jack quickly adds, "Then our son Rob told me over the phone the wonderful news of his salvation!" Shortly thereafter, Rob and Guia made a covenant in marriage before the Lord. In addition, Jack and Martha's prayer request for their grandchildren's spiritual growth was answered. "Now they go to Sunday school, church clubs and young people's!" Jack gratefully exclaims.

Christmas is truly a time of great meaning and joy for the Hiebert family now that the Lord Jesus is at the centre of their lives and their celebration! —KS

❧ *13* ❧

Kathy Peel

Parenting God's Way

Kathy Peel is a busy lady. As the author of ten books which, combined, have sold 1,000,000 copies, she is on the staff of *Family Circle* and writes regular columns for *Aspire* and *Release Ink* magazines.

As founder and president of Creative People Incorporated and the Family Manager, she is committed to providing helpful resources to strengthen busy families.

Kathy and her husband Bill have three sons. Having battled chronic fatigue syndrome for two years, Kathy realized that she could not be the kind of wife, mother, and friend she needed to be without the supernatural, empowering strength of God.

Amid the busyness of her life, she and Bill set aside six Monday morning dates in a coffee shop to decide what values they wanted to teach their kids. Having determined that the Ten Commandments are as relevant for parenting today's children as they have ever been, they decided that the "do nots" would be followed by the "dos" in their approach. Thus, "Do not covet," would be followed by, "Do be thankful." Likewise, "Be a giver," would follow, "Do not steal."

During the six dates, Kathy and Bill concluded that it was not what they would *leave* their kids that was important, but the values they would *impart* to them.

They committed to listening to their children's music (including reading the lyrics), watching their favourite TV shows, and in general, being in touch with the influences in their lives. By helping them to discern the sources, Kathy and Bill would prepare them for the teen years when they would begin making their own decisions.

From Kathy and Bill's discussions, four "I"s of parenting emerged: 1) Incarnation, 2) Indoctrination, 3) Initiation, and 4) Immersion.

Incarnation refers to the living out of a parent's values. Kathy illustrates this point with the story of her speeding. When she got a ticket, she had to take responsibility for her wrongdoing and apologize. Kids know that parents make mistakes and are more authentic if they are transparent and repent of their own wrongs.

Indoctrination refers to the teaching aspect of parenting. In order to be effective within the context of a family, there needs to be a sense of enjoyment in learning and fun in teaching. Family devotions are foundational to instilling reasons for positive behaviour and the development of balanced Christian living. Praying with children communicates the reality of talking and listening to God on a regular basis.

Initiation is the stage at which children are encouraged to try out the values they are being taught. It's important not to shelter children in the sense of smothering them, but rather to encourage them to live and learn and occasionally fail in the presence of their parents, where they have an opportunity to correct errors in judgement. The message needs to be, "I don't necessarily agree with the choices you've made, but I still love you." Love must be unconditional, even in failure.

Love must be unconditional.

Immersion refers to the environment of love and consistent spiritual values which surround a child in everyday life. A child who is immersed in a solid value system will escape much of the confusion which frustrates so many today.

Kathy and Bill view the Bible as the "Operating Manual" for life and believe that God changes the world through individuals. "Strong people build strong families; strong families build strong communities; strong communities build strong cultures; strong cultures build strong countries."

Through all of her research and experience, Kathy has learned the importance of laughter, a quality she stresses in her written work, her seminars, her parenting, and most particularly in her marriage. Kathy's books include:

- *The Mother's Survival Trilogy*
- *Do Plastic Surgeons Take Visa?*
- *The Stomach Virus and Other Forms of Family Bonding*
- *The Little Book of Family Joys* —DRL

It's not what you leave to your children but what you leave in them.

❧ *14* ❧

Joey & Laura Messenger

Fishing for Souls

In a small fishing village off the east coast, live Joey and Laura Messenger. Surrounding them are several beautiful beaches located along the island's shores – only minutes from their home.

Growing up on the island has provided Joey with many memories. He recalls sharing his first experiences as a fisherman/lobsterman with his father, who was captain of the crew. Following in his father's footsteps, Joey also decided to make a living in the fishing industry.

On a typical day during the fishing season, Joey, along with his captain and four fellow crewmen, launch out into the vast waters of the Atlantic in hopes of getting a good catch for the day. Evident to his friends aboard, is Joey's close walk with the Lord as he willingly shares his faith when the opportunity arises.

Meanwhile at home, Laura, a busy mother of two boys – John and Sean – plans out the events of her day. Besides her role as wife and mother, she is also on the committee of a women's outreach program in the community and assists with the Sunday school program of their church.

As Laura and the children sit around the kitchen table, young John eagerly leads out in prayer for God's blessing upon the meal. It is during moments like these, Laura is reminded of God's intervention in their lives.

While watching *100 Huntley Street* several years ago, Joey and Laura listened intently as Grant Jeffrey and the late John Wesley White discussed the book of Revelation. Although not a

Christian at the time, Joey was always fascinated with this topic. Laura, too, was intrigued and began to search for more answers to the unveiling mysteries of God's Word. During the program, they each prayed the sinner's prayer quietly in their own hearts. Afterwards when they shared their decision with one another, Joey and Laura realized that they both accepted the Lord at the same time!

While praying the sinner's prayer, Joey sensed a change taking place deep within his heart. He describes it in his own words: "It felt as if tons of weight and pressure had been lifted. All the guilt and hate I had carried vanished away."

When Joey's parents came over for a visit, they immediately noticed a difference in Laura's countenance. After she explained the events that had taken place concerning their salvation, her mother-in-law commented, "I can see it in your face!"

In reference to Joey and Laura's spiritual progress, Pastor Don Smith says, "It's amazing to see their growth and dedication to the work of God. They are fine examples of Christians, and their love of the Lord is evident to all." —KS

15

Jerry Johnston

Preventing Teen Suicide

Slowly, Jerry Johnston walked to the kitchen entryway and picked up the telephone receiver. Mechanically, he dialed his father's office. "Dad, this is Jerry. I'm going to kill myself."

With his mother an alcoholic, Jerry had become a burned out drug user caught up in the party lifestyle. Finally, the only thing that seemed to make any sense was death. But God had other ideas. Jerry didn't kill himself that day, but instead, found himself some time later at a Christian camp. The Gospel message revolutionized his life. With a burden for his friends, he went on to prepare his life for ministry.

Today, Jerry is an internationally recognized evangelist, known for his ability to bridge the generation gap and speak in a manner relevant to our modern culture. With over 20 years in ministry, he has spoken to more than three million students in school assemblies and is the author of several books: *Why Suicide?; The Edge of Evil; How to Save Your Kids From Ruin;* and *The Last Days of Planet Earth.*

With three children of his own and an intimate understanding of the pressures of adolescence, Jerry was deeply grieved a few years ago when a friend's daughter hung herself. While the girl's parents had meant well, their approach to guidance had been too heavy-handed. Overwhelmed, the daughter opted out – leaving everyone utterly devastated.

Why Suicide? is Jerry's attempt to protect both parents and kids from the horrors of self-inflicted death. In this book, he gives an excellent overview of the "epidemic" of teenage suicide, clarifying the prominent reasons why kids take their own lives and clearly outlining the warning signs. He identifies eight important steps for its avoidance:

1. Start listening.
2. Be discerning.
3. Teach with love.
4. Embrace your kids.
5. Monitor friends.
6. Model the message.
7. Care enough to correct.
8. Pray with your kids. —DRL

The family that prays together, stays together.

∼ 16 ∼

Evelyn Knudson

The Power of God's Love

"You're no good, and you'll never amount to anything!" Evelyn Knudson could still hear these piercing words as clearly as she did the day they were spoken. And although many years had transpired since then, the memories of the abuse she received as a child seemed to bombard her thoughts relentlessly. Looking for an easy way out, she contemplated suicide.

"It was during the spring of 1984. My husband Duane and I had just recently moved onto an acreage. Although we were running two businesses and were very busy, my life was empty. I felt that nobody cared and nobody loved me," she confides. "All my childhood hurts kept haunting me."

Living in the country only intensified her feelings of isolation and rejection. However, God heard Evelyn's cry of desperation and was able to minister personally to her needs through Christian television.

"That particular morning when I turned on *100 Huntley Street*, I was lonely and very, very down. Amazingly, David Mainse was speaking to people who were hurting and lonely. He explained that Jesus was there to fill that loneliness. His message over the airwaves really began tugging at my heart."

Gently, the Lord helped Evelyn to understand the need of forgiveness, and the important role it has in the healing process. "God dealt with me bit by bit," she explains. "I have actually been able to lay all my childhood hurts down and forgive everyone who has hurt me."

While this deep transformation was taking place, the Lord began to work on the rest of the family. Willingly Duane took Evelyn to church every Sunday. In fact, he was glad to get back into the routine of attending himself. Of his childhood, he says, "I had a very good upbringing in the home. My family all went to church pretty well every Sunday."

Eventually, with exposure to the Word of God through attending church on Sunday and watching *100 Huntley Street* during the week, Duane also recognized his need of accepting Christ as Saviour. In addition, their youngest son Neil came to know the Lord through the ministry of Circle Square Ranch!

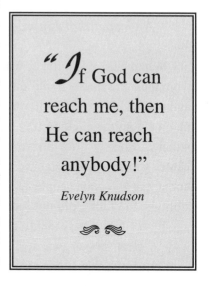

> "*If* God can reach me, then He can reach anybody!"
>
> *Evelyn Knudson*

The Godly foundation that Duane and Evelyn had laid in the home also impacted their other two children. As a result, their eldest son Don is a wonderful husband and father today, and their daughter Joanne is wholeheartedly serving the Lord!

Duane and Evelyn are thankful to God, not only for His blessings on them and their children, but on their grandchildren as well! And their once empty lives are now full of new meaning and joy as they serve Him.

Although they have had their share of challenges, Duane and Evelyn have learned the importance of depending on the Lord to meet their every need. And He has proven Himself mighty. Evelyn concludes by saying, "The power of God's love over the airwaves can reach the unreachable. If He can reach me, then He can reach anybody!" —KS

⊸ *17* ⊶

Elmer Whittaker

A Gospel that Embraces the Totality of Man's Need

When Elmer Whittaker was about to be born, his father ran from their log shanty to the shed, hitched up the horse and buggy, and rushed his swollen wife to Athabaska. In 1947, there were no medical facilities in their tiny black community of Amber Valley, Alberta. Shortly after arriving at the hospital, the horse died. Elmer and his twin sister were born into such an impoverished home that the poor people called them poor folk. With six other siblings, the future did not look bright for the two new babies.

Elmer was a very sickly child, but his mother, though poor, was a great prayer warrior, rich in the things of the Lord. Consequently, it was no surprise that God's hand was mightily on the boy. He accepted Jesus when very young.

At 12 years of age, his eyes were opened to see something that few people ever see. There, standing beside his bed, was an angel. The glory filled the room and Elmer became aware of the realm of the Spirit in a way that has never left him.

As a teenager in high school, Elmer was so aware of the presence of God walking with him up and down the hallways, that the teachers called him aside to see what was happening to him. Thinking that he was experiencing some problems, they had no idea that he was simply enjoying the company of his Heavenly Father. Following graduation, Elmer received a Masters Electrician License and started his own electrical contracting company in 1974. With Godly principles of good stewardship firmly entrenched, he became very successful, employing 27 people.

Through it all, Elmer did not forget God. For 17 years, he and his wife Maxine were faithful members of Edmonton Faith Temple, where they served in practically every facet of ministry, from janitorial to praise and worship leadership, to the positions of senior elders. Elmer had overcome a sickly childhood, extreme poverty and the racial issue. In the process, he had found self-sufficiency. Now it was time for God to take him to the next step – all-sufficiency in Christ.

In 1979, Elmer and Maxine went on a three-week singing tour to Jamaica. During the trip, Elmer began to sense that God was calling him into full-time ministry. Within a week, this direction was confirmed by a prophetic utterance during a crusade meeting. In 1980, Elmer was ordained by Faith Temple and began part-time evangelistic work. Within four years, Bethel Bible Fellowship was born with 41 people and quickly expanded to accommodate over 500, 80 percent of whom are first-generation Christians.

The ministry of Bethel takes place through the power of the Holy Spirit and focusses on every aspect of man's need – whether spiritual, physical, financial, emotional or social. God is recognized as the Source. Life is not categorized into spiritual and temporal realms, but is recognized as entirely spiritual. Thus, Elmer and Maxine work extensively together with single mothers, the homeless and the unemployed. They run a drop-in centre two blocks from the local high school and staff it with volunteers. They continuously make job referrals and have an excellent success rate of making provision for the full spectrum of life issues. In short, Bethel preaches a "Gospel that embraces the totality of man's need."

While God's leading has been mightily evidenced in Elmer's life, his faith has been greatly tested with regard to his health. Each time, however, he and Maxine have faced the tests as opportunities to see the healing hand of God. Following a diagnosis of bowel cancer, Elmer went to preach in India. Instead of losing weight as the doctors predicted, he held on to the Word and gained. Upon his return, a visit to the specialist determined no sign of cancer! As the Great Physician, God has overcome every time. Not much wonder that their church is often referred to as a "hospital." —DRL

Trials and experiences mature us. God is stretching people so they will learn to trust Him.

❧ 18 ❧

Ann Rollins

Changed from the Inside Out!

The words of the rock song reverberated over the loud speaker: "I can't get no satisfaction...." And even though everyone at the party appeared to be having fun while under the influence of alcohol and drugs, Ann Rollins knew deep down inside that these words contained an element of truth. "I searched in every corner of the world it seemed," she says. "I tried everything – yoga, reading horoscopes, and all kinds of junk like that. Nothing satisfied me. Alcohol didn't do it; drugs didn't do it; dancing, parties, late nights and singing my heart out until two or three in the morning didn't do it. Absolutely nothing the world had to offer brought me satisfaction."

The use of drugs and alcohol couldn't remove the emotional pain or memories of the abuse Ann experienced as a child, nor did it lessen the devastation she felt over the breakup of her parents' marriage.

Years earlier, in an attempt to escape from the past, Ann married a man who became an alcoholic: "I was very, very young. I had four children by the time I was 20. We were both drinkers, and we performed musically at parties, nightclubs and weddings where alcohol was easily accessible. When I left him, I took my children and away I went. Raising four children without any financial support from my ex-husband made life so unbearable that I found comfort in drinking. This continued for years. I even began to bootleg liquor and drink on the job (I kept a pint in my purse). My life was really messed up. That's when I started getting heavily into drugs."

Eventually, Ann was forced to face the dangers of this lifestyle. "Two of my friends were found dead due to an accidental drug overdose," she states sadly. "My life was also on a road of destruction with the abuse of alcohol and prescription drugs, but I couldn't find a way out. It just seemed like there was no end to the road I was on."

Then there was news of an upcoming *100 Huntley Street* rally in town, and one of Ann's friends invited her to attend. She listened intently as a man gave his testimony about how he had been saved and delivered from alcoholism. Afterwards, when David Mainse gave the invitation to receive Jesus Christ as Saviour, Ann knew beyond a shadow of a doubt that this was what she needed to do. "When I heard the invitation to be born again – to ask Jesus into my heart – that was the clincher. David explained it in such a way that I was the first one at the altar!"

Shortly after this life-changing experience, Ann began her journey along a different road. She discovered the joy and wonder of having a personal relationship with Jesus. "A few weeks after accepting the Lord, I received the baptism of the Holy Spirit. It was absolutely phenomenal! On Mother's Day of that same year, I got baptized in water! And I've never looked back. I just kept going forward."

Since January 20, 1980 – the day Ann received Jesus as her Saviour – life has taken on a whole new meaning. She now uses every opportunity available to reach others for Him – in prisons, in nursing homes and on the streets. And she knows from experience that nothing else in life can bring greater satisfaction! — KS

⤳ *19* ⤳

Joanne Wallace

A Woman Who Wins

From all appearances, Joanne Wallace had it all. She was beautiful, charming, intelligent and had received a strong foundation for her life in a solid Christian family. Despite struggling with normal confusion in her teens, she had recognized the road from misery to joy in her early 20s and dedicated her life to Jesus.

As a professional model, and chosen Mrs. Oregon in 1969, Joanne was a competitor in the Mrs. America Pageant. Her early married life to a man she adored was filled with all the glamour and excitement of which most young wives can only dream. Wanting to help other young women to achieve their full potential, Joanne formed the internationally recognized Image Improvement Incorporated. Interviewed by scores of talk show hosts, she became not only a media darling, but the head of a Christian-based corporation.

Unfortunately, no benefit earth has to offer can guarantee a bump free ride on life's road. Just when Joanne thought that her life was progressing in an exemplary way, the wheel came off.

Within 30 days, she was sued and faced both financial failure and the ruin of her marriage. While such circumstances are devastating for anyone, for someone in a ministry position, they are doubly painful as the precious message of Christ becomes threatened with reproach.

As the details of destruction invaded the most tender places of Joanne's heart, and divorce became an unavoidable blot on her life, the grief was so great that she thought she would die. Depression became her constant companion – there to torment her in the night watches; there to mock her at the moment of waking.

During those nightmarish days, the one constant that sustained Joanne was the weekly Bible study group where her friends allowed her to cry, held her, refrained from preaching, ministered healing and, when they could offer no helpful words, simply showed up the following morning to take her to breakfast.

As tilled soil must defer to life springing forth from a dead seed, the barrenness of Joanne's soul gradually gave way to the freshening of Jesus. Tiny sprouts of compassion for others who have gone through similar things began to emerge and her heart was filled with tenderness for them.

Now, with books and cassettes on inner and outer beauty, Joanne is a best-selling author, media personality, internationally known speaker, former corporation president – as well as wife (for the second time), mother and grandmother to her family. Although she continues to give seminars on personal improvement to men and women around the world, she knows that the key to her effectiveness is the depth of love for people that she gained through her painful loss. —DRL

The most powerful person is one who prays. Although I can't control my circumstances, I can control my reaction or response.

⊶ *20* ⊷

John & Helen Burns

A Flame Rekindled

Lively music and joyful songs of praise express the hearts of almost 1,400 people as they gather together to worship the Lord. As pastors of the Victory Christian Centre in Vancouver, John and Helen Burns are grateful for all the wonderful things God has done in the lives of their entire family, and also for the people of their community and beyond.

With a sparkle in her eyes, Helen reminisces back to her teenage years when she first met her high school sweetheart, John, the middle linebacker of the football team. When John discovered that Helen was a "born again" Christian, he curiously opened up the subject of God. Helen's exuberant response about her faith touched his heart. Very soon after, he too, received the Lord Jesus Christ as his personal Saviour.

Three weeks after they got married, John was accepted into the Faculty of Dentistry at the University of British Columbia. Helen describes it as a very exciting time: "It seemed like the world was big and wonderful since everything was going for us."

Over the next few years, however, these high school sweethearts began to slowly drift away from the Lord and from each other. In assessment of the real problem, Helen confides, "I can remember praying, 'God, what happened?' Then I realized, it certainly wasn't God that blew it. If anything was wrong, it was something I let go of. I didn't have the active faith that I had as a teenager working in my life anymore."

Upon this realization, Helen got on her knees and prayed, "Lord, I don't want to live without You anymore. Please forgive me. I need to have the relationship that I once had with You. I want John and I to serve You together and our children to know You."

With a hunger for the things of God, Helen began watching *100 Huntley Street* which she refers to as her "lifeline," for it kept her in touch with the Word of God and began to evoke changes in her marriage.

At the same time, God was at work in John's life. When his dental practice schedule permitted a morning coffee break, he would hurry home to watch *100 Huntley Street* with Helen and the girls. The program was also instrumental in the salvation of their daughters when they were young children. And this is not all God has done....

The Lord has wrought other miracles in and through their lives. With the infilling of the Holy Spirit and God's healing touch upon his stuttering, John began to share the Gospel with others. Doors of ministry opened up for Helen as well. Eventually, God spoke to both their hearts about the need of beginning a church in their area, which He has abundantly blessed for the past several years.

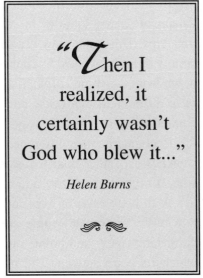

"*Then* I realized, it certainly wasn't God who blew it..."

Helen Burns

Ministering to the needs of others is truly a family affair, for each member of the Burns family is actively involved in reaching the unsaved through church ministry, television broadcasting and special youth outreach programs. "Christian television plays a powerful role," John acknowledges. "It changes the spiritual complexion of a society, and we need a lot more of it!" —KS

✎ *21* ✎

Dr. Gary Chapman

The Five Love Languages

Dr. Gary Chapman directs marriage seminars throughout the country and counsels married couples regularly. With over twenty years of experience, he has written some excellent resource books: *Towards a Growing Marriage; Hope for the Separated; Building Relationships;* and *The Five Love Languages.*

In this most recent book, *The Five Love Languages,* Dr. Chapman shares some of his most important insights on relationships. This book grew out of his concern that many couples simply don't know how to connect emotionally. Once they come down from the "high" of "falling in love," and discover that they have differences that cause conflict, they need to learn how to communicate in a healthy way.

Recognizing the differences as balances of strengths and weaknesses, rather than focussing on them as sources of division, is crucial to positive relationships.

With his wealth of experience, Dr. Chapman has identified five basic ways that people communicate. He calls these the "love languages" and points out that there are many dialects in which they are spoken. The number of ways to express love within a love language is limited only by one's imagination.

It is very important for people to understand what language of love their partners are speaking. Most often, whatever they complain about or request most frequently reveals the love language of the person. For instance, if a woman uses words of affirmation to her husband, she wants words of affirmation in return.

The Five Love Languages are:

1. *Words of Affirmation* – The use of words to build up and encourage the other person. This is not commonly a male love language as men are not usually as good with words of affirmation as are women.
2. *Quality Time* – Giving each other undivided attention.
3. *Receiving Gifts* – Gift-giving should be a part of the marriage process and does not need to be expensive to be effective.
4. *Acts of Service* – Doing things for the other person.
5. *Physical Touch* – Holding hands, embracing, sexual intimacy, physical affection, etc. —DRL

God gave the gift of His Son and He touched people. Now He wants to spend time with us.

❧ 22 ❧

Helen Guenther

Love Doesn't Count the Cost

As 16-year-old Helen Guenther got ready for school that morning of June '93, the warm rays of sunlight cascaded through the window. It was a reminder to her that summer vacation was only a matter of days away.

Hurrying out the front door with textbooks in hand, Helen proceeded to walk the usual route to school. Unknown to her, a man was lurking outside the quiet court where she resided. Suddenly, without warning, the stranger lurched toward her in an unwarranted attack. The following blur of events that took place was enough to severely traumatize Helen for days, months and even years to come.

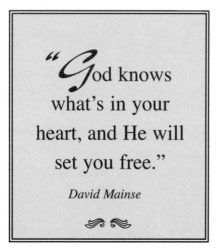

"God knows what's in your heart, and He will set you free."

David Mainse

"No one would expect to be attacked in broad daylight," Helen states. "After the assault, I went straight home. My older brother sensed something was wrong. So I told him what happened, and he immediately called the police."

With brokenness in her voice, she continues to recount that most horrifying day of her life: "My mom came down to the police station with me. It was so hard.... I was still in a state of shock and couldn't identify my attacker very well, even though he came right in front of me. This meant the police didn't have enough evidence to go on."

The injustice left her feeling very angry and remorseful. Then two weeks later, when hearing the news of another young girl who had been assaulted in the same area, Helen felt it was more than she could bear.

Due to the nature of the crime, there was also a terrible sense of isolation. With tears, she says, "I wanted to tell somebody but I was just too ashamed. So I kept it all inside – except for my parents and my brother. I was afraid to tell my friends. I thought they wouldn't understand or they wouldn't believe me."

Being alienated from others only heightened her anger and pain. Within months of the incident, Helen sank deeper and deeper into a severe depression. Soon suicidal thoughts began to overtake this once carefree, happy young teen.

One day, as Helen stood in the middle of the kitchen, holding the knife to her wrist, a ferocious battle took place within. Although it was a close call, she came to the conclusion that taking her life was not the answer. But how was she to deal with the endless torment and pain?

"My parents had been watching *100 Huntley Street* for many years," she recalls. "By the time I was 19, I was watching the program myself. That day (ironically, it was in June), David Mainse gave an invitation for those who wanted to come to the Lord. It was a simple prayer. He then explained, 'God knows what's in your heart, and He will set you free of whatever you are going through.' Right then, I felt as if a big burden had been lifted off my heart – the burden I had been carrying for three years. It was such a relief – like I had never experienced before. I finally had peace and joy in my heart which I hadn't had in so long."

And the changes that took place that day have given Helen a whole new perspective as well. Instantly, the feelings of contempt, anger and bitterness she harboured toward the stranger who assaulted her were replaced with compassion and an enormous concern for his soul.

"Now my heart really goes out to those who commit crimes and hurt innocent people," she says with conviction. "I believe so many (perpetrators) are hurting because they didn't get love. They feel that nobody cares...."

And Helen is determined to do something positive about it! She knows from personal experience the importance of sharing God's love and the need to bring His salvation and healing to others. "Like the lyrics of a song by Ricky Skaggs and Billy Dean, 'When it comes to love, you don't count the cost.'" —KS

✍ *23* ✍

Carol Lawrence

From Broadway to a TBN Talk Show

The original "Maria" in *West Side Story,* Carol Lawrence is an actress, singer, talk show host for the Trinity Broadcasting Network (TBN) and business woman. With more credits for screen roles, live concert performances and live theatre than could possibly be mentioned here, Carol has long been a household name in the entertainment industry.

For many years, she was married to Robert Goulet, with whom she had two sons, Michael and Christopher, who have both appeared with her in concerts and on TV. When interviewed on *100 Huntley Street*, Carol spoke briefly about the role alcohol played in the failure of her marriage.

Despite the glamour surrounding celebrities, no one is exempt from the challenges of humanity. It is the difficulties which God allows in every life that are most often the catalyst through which people reach out to Him. Through the death of Carol's mother, with whom she was very close, and the struggles of single parenting, she found God to be her refuge and strength.

In promoting her book, *I Remember Pasta,* Carol reflected on her Italian heritage, her love of life, and her mother's wonderful four-course spaghetti meals. She loved the special times with her family over long dinners.

With such rich family memories, Carol now encourages other families to get involved with the cooking in their homes. With everyone pitching in, doing a little of this and a little of that, sprinkling a little love here and some chatter there, a pinch of laughter here and some salty conversation there, the family grows to be very close. Mixing up things that are fun and delicious at the same time makes for an unforgettable smorgasbord of memories.

A longtime children's advocate, Carol has hosted many telethons for needy children. Her volunteer work for World Vision has been invaluable in raising millions of dollars for children in Third World countries. Now, through *The Carol Lawrence Show,* her own weekly magazine/talk show which she writes and produces for TBN, Carol features celebrities, cooking, nutrition, fashion, exercise, children, music and other topics, all within a Christian context. Little wonder that her vitality and energy has won her recognition as the City of Hope's Woman of the Year (1996), as well as the Spirit of Life and Angel awards.
—DRL

We've forgotten the relationships we develop over the dinner table.

❧ 24 ❧

Bernice Erickson & Kyla

Focussing On Jesus

Years ago, Bernice Erickson had never given much thought to God. Yet, despite the fact that everything in her life was seemingly good, she always had a sense of being "lost" and empty. However, the turning point for Bernice took place in 1978 when her two-year-old granddaughter, Kyla, was diagnosed with cancer in the retina of her eye. The medical team did all they could to save her eye, yet without success.

Bernice experienced emotional pain and suffering as she helplessly stood by. Once again, Kyla was to begin another series of chemotherapy, radiation and cryopexy (laser treatment), in vain effort to save the other eye.

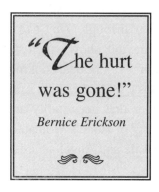

"*The* hurt was gone!"

Bernice Erickson

By the time Kyla was four years old, doctors feared the risk of losing her while surgically removing the other eye and 20 cancerous tumours.

The day Kyla was scheduled for surgery, Bernice waited anxiously at home. In the midst of her anguish, she tuned to *100 Huntley Street*. Something David Mainse said caught her attention, and she knew that God was speaking to her heart. As David invited viewers to accept Christ as their Saviour, Bernice decided to pray along with him.

She recalls this life-changing event: "As I said those words, still weeping, something happened. A warmth came over me. The hurt was gone! The Lord Jesus took it away and I had the most beautiful peace...."

The day Bernice accepted the Lord was only the beginning. The testimonies and daily teaching on *100 Huntley Street* enabled her to grow spiritually while strengthening her faith in God. With the joy of knowing Jesus personally, Bernice couldn't keep the wonderful news to herself. Soon, one by one, little Kyla and the rest of the family also turned their lives over to the Lord.

God's blessing upon them is evident today. As a high school graduate, Kyla has never allowed her blindness to hinder her. And what is the motivating factor in Kyla's life? Like her grandmother, she has a genuine love for the Lord. She attributes this to the encouragement received from her family and Circle Square Ranch where she has learned the importance of keeping her focus on Jesus. —KS

❧ *25* ❧

Lee Ezell

A Tapestry of Grace

Childhood abuse at the hands of alcoholic parents and rape by a co-worker were the background colours of the tapestry of Lee Ezell's life. Interwoven among the threads were dark tones, like the pregnancy resulting from the rape while she was yet a virgin. The shocking thing, as one looks at Lee's life, is the brilliance of wit, resiliency and laughter, all merging in magnificent harmony as a masterpiece of God's perfect design.

One would wonder why God would allow such painful things to happen to a beautiful, innocent young girl. Yet without the dark tones, the brilliance of God's grace would have been lost. While Lee's story contains so many elements of genuine tragedy, not a vestige of victimization emerges. Lee claims that "a victim is a *yesterday* person, trying to get along with a *today* God, who has great plans for *tomorrow!*"

As a teenager in 1961, Lee attended a Billy Graham Crusade in Philadelphia and committed her life to Christ. Amazingly, it was during that time of Christian growth that the rape occurred, leading to a deeper walk with Christ.

When Lee discovered that she was pregnant, she had no thought of abortion and withstood the nine months of pregnancy in valiant preparation for the adoption of the baby. All through the years, Lee prayed for the precious baby girl (her only natural child) she had not been able to keep.

One day, 35 years later, there was a phone call. The result was the indescribable reunion of Lee with her beautiful daughter Julie. God had answered Lee's prayers for her in every way.

Raised by wonderful Christian parents, Julie had grown up to be a well-adjusted, healthy, bright girl who loved God and held no bitterness in her heart. During their first meeting, Julie's husband Bob thanked Lee for giving birth to Julie rather than aborting her. It was a very moving moment. Audiences and readers throughout the world have been transfixed by the unfolding story as both have appeared on such programs as *The Sally Show, Geraldo, Oprah* and *Donahue*. The story has been the subject of many magazine articles.

Lee's most recent book, *Will the Real Me Please Stand Up,* is an amusing, yet deeply insightful guide to personal growth. She outlines five steps to finding the "real you":

1. *Receive the truth.*
2. *Remove the layers.* Forgiveness each step of the way is essential. According to Lee, if you don't forgive people, you are allowing them to live rent-free in your head.
3. *Review the present.* If you have a real friend who knows the real you, ask that person for an assessment of your present approach to life.
4. *Risk revealing the real you.* Many people are so afraid of rejection that they stay hidden behind self-imposed walls. It may never have occurred to them that their inadequacy is their first qualification for being used by God.
5. *Reflect your Redeemer.* Remove the veil. Older women often find it harder to be open and honest. The real you is God's gift to you. What you do with it is your gift to God.

Lee now travels as a "humour therapist," helping people to find "God's peace for their 'missing pieces' in life." With a wealth of examples from her own life, she illustrates the ability of Christ to fill in the gaps and redeem "crummy" situations. With radiance, she encourages people into new hope in the faithfulness of a loving God who is able to make all things work together for good. Her other books include: *The Missing Piece*, her story of rape, pregnancy, adoption and reunion; and *The Cinderella Syndrome.* —DRL

If Satan is living rent-free in your head, evict that sucker! Get him out of there! (2 Cor. 3:18).

∾ 26 ∾

Rev. Bob Rumball

Worthy of Double Honour
(1 Timothy 5:17)

Over the years, Morley and Helen Thomson carefully watched the life of Rev. Bob Rumball, a former CFL football player and an energetic man of God. Rev. Rumball strongly believes that there is nothing a person cannot do, especially with the enabling of the Lord. He has proven this Scriptural truth many times throughout his ministry and personal life.

In appreciation of Rev. Rumball's fine Godly example and inspiration, Morley and Helen decided to purchase a Crossroads Walk of Faith stone in his honour. It was engraved and symbolically placed during the *100 Huntley Street* program on October 27, 1994.

Morley speaks highly of Rev. Rumball, who presently serves as chaplain for the Metropolitan Toronto Police Association, making mention of his many outstanding accomplishments – especially concerning his tremendous involvement with the Deaf community.

After graduating from seminary in the spring of '52, Rev. Rumball expressed his willingness to accept the call of ministering to the Deaf, provided he was able to learn sign language in one month. To everyone's amazement, he quickly mastered this new language within his stipulated time frame. He then knew, without a doubt, that the Lord's direction for him was to accept the post as pastor of the Evangelical Church of the Deaf, the only church for the Deaf in the city of Toronto at the time.

> *"Therefore, My beloved brethren, be steadfast, immovable, always abounding in the work of the Lord, knowing that your labour is not in vain in the Lord."*
>
> *1 Corinthians 15:58*

With a strong commitment in this area of ministry, Rev. Rumball also initiated the construction of a centre in Toronto, which was founded in 1979. In his very active role over the years as Executive Director of *The Bob Rumball Centre for the Deaf*, he has pioneered ministries for the Deaf in other provinces and countries (Jamaica and Puerto Rico), founded a year-round camp and conference centre, and established a foster home program consisting of nine group homes.

His immovable, unwavering faith was demonstrated even when circumstances seemed hopeless. Morley recalls an incident that took place several years ago when Rev. Rumball accidentally severed his first two fingers while woodworking. Although told by medical staff it would be impossible, Rev. Rumball insisted they rejoin his fingers because he needed them when ministering to the Deaf. The endeavour to save his severed fingers proved successful, thus enabling him to continue preaching and ministering to the needs of people through sign language.

Along with his vision to win lost souls for Christ by preaching the Gospel through sign language, Rev. Rumball has a compelling desire to meet the practical needs of the Deaf. This led him to invent a portable telephone device for the Deaf, which was honoured and utilized by the Bell Canada telephone company in 1972. As a result of his accomplishments on behalf of the Deaf, Rev. Rumball has had many doors open for him to minister all over the world. Yet, despite his extremely busy schedule, he makes a point of being available to individuals in times of need. Whether it means taking the time to talk with a family member or represent a Deaf person in court, Rev. Rumball believes in making the most of every opportunity.

This genuine concern for others is shared by his wife Mary Jean, who has always been a backbone to him and the ministry. As parents of four children of their own, they have also included an adopted child and a foster child in their family.

The Scripture engraved on the Walk of Faith stone that has been chosen in honour of Rev. (Dr.) Bob and Mary Jean Rumball is found in 1 Corinthians 15:58: *"Therefore, My beloved brethren, be steadfast, immovable, always abounding in the work of the Lord, knowing that your labour is not in vain in the Lord."*
—KS

✐ 27 ✐

Duane Miller

A New Voice for Jesus

Duane Miller loved to preach – and people loved to hear him. As pastor of the large (24,000) First Baptist Church in Brenham, Texas, he had plenty of opportunity. Next to preaching, he loved to sing. Many remember him touring as part of a quartet in music evangelism throughout the United States and Canada.

Prior to his appointment in Brenham, Duane was the Young Adult director and Sunday school teacher at Houston's First Baptist Church. According to the senior pastor, he was indispensable. "Duane served as the church's putty; if there was a need, he filled it."

Four years after moving to Brenham, Duane got the flu – but this wasn't just any old flu. The virus penetrated the nerves of his vocal chords and rendered them useless.

Because it was so unusual, 63 doctors from all over the world exhaustively examined and documented Duane's condition, to the extent that he felt "like a human guinea pig." They were all baffled. Month by month, they took scopes on video of his vocal chords and could not understand why they seemed to have been destroyed. When all was said and done, however, they gave him no hope of recovery, leaving him not only very discouraged, but exceedingly frustrated.

For over three years, Duane could not be heard above a whisper. This necessitated his resignation as pastor of the Brenham church.

Refusing to give up on life or on his desire to teach the Word of God, Duane went back to his old church in Houston. With the assistance of special microphones and amplifying equipment, coupled with tremendous effort on his part, he learned to communicate verbally. With the blessing of his pastor, he accepted an assignment to teach his old Sunday school class, a microphone perched on his lip. With love and patience, the class of 200 learned to understand the low, raspy sound. For Duane, it took so much effort that he was soaked with sweat at the conclusion of every lesson.

From time to time, Duane's discouragement was so profound that he questioned God. He could not understand why, when he was so willing to be used for the kingdom, God would not heal his vocal chords. There were times when he felt deeply hurt.

In an attempt to make lemonade out of his lemon, and faced with the prospect of never speaking again, Duane decided that it would be a good opportunity to begin the book he had long intended to write. He queried several publishers, but was rewarded only with rejection, citing his inability to speak as a deterrent to his ability to promote his work. Now devastated and confused, Duane was at the end of himself.

Three days after receiving the rejection letter from the publisher, it was Sunday. As was his habit, he dressed for church and made final preparations for his class. That day, he would speak on the 103rd Psalm.

As Duane stood before his class that day, he whispered raspily of God's marvellous redemption and healing. As he pushed the words out against the windscreen, trickles of perspiration streaming from his brow, his thoughts went to his own condition. But why not me? he questioned. Why not me?

As the video camera and the audio tape rolled, recording the lesson, something began to happen. Duane's voice began to return! Slowly at first, then with increasing strength, he could speak again! He and the class were astonished! They knew they were witnessing the proof that God's Word was true – right before their eyes!

The next day, Duane called his doctor for an appointment, the first in a series of "show and tell" sessions with amazed doctors who had no explanation for any of it – including the disappearance of all scar tissue that had been growing over the three-year period. According to Duane, the scar tissue was like sin: "It's there – then it's gone when you trust in God."

These days, Duane is Executive Director of New Voice Ministries and is committed to serving God through communication, motivation and facilitation. Through his programs, he communicates the relevance of the Gospel of Jesus Christ to life today. He encourages individuals to action in personal ministry and contribution to the needs of others. —DRL

God puts us through the agony of waiting so our faith is rooted more deeply in Him.

❧ 28 ❧

James MacDonald

The Transforming Power of God

Throngs of people have assembled to hear the fiery young evangelist preach the Gospel. With holy boldness he proclaims, "We serve a miracle-working God!" Several nod in agreement, especially those who have witnessed the transforming power of God in the life of this modern-day apostle.

Prior to his dramatic conversion to Christianity, James MacDonald was known in local Native communities as a "hopeless town drunk." Often his drinking binges would last for several weeks, causing frequent blackouts and lapses of memory.

"There were times I blacked out for three days," he admits. "I would awaken to find myself crawling around in a ditch by the road or in the grass of a field somewhere. It was just a horrible life."

The roots of alcoholism began in early childhood. By the time James was ready to enter high school, he had already become accustomed to the drinking lifestyle. Even a close encounter with death was not enough to deter this headstrong teenager: "I was rushed to the hospital once because I overdosed on alcohol. Yet, after having this close call, I continued drinking."

When James received the tragic news of his father's murder in 1978, his drinking binges and eventual drug use increased, and so did the eruptions of his anger. Soon the new church next door became the target of his violent outbursts. "I was doing a lot of crazy things," he explains, "like causing havoc and fights in the middle of the sermons. I was totally in a demonic rage because of my heavy use of alcohol and drugs."

Ironically, it was during the odd hours of the night that many of the town drunks tuned into Life-Changing Television, and James happened to be one of them.

"We only had one TV channel at the time, and *100 Huntley Street* was the only ministry that was on. I would wonder who this Jesus was that they were talking about. Under the conviction of the Holy Spirit, tears would come to my eyes. But because I didn't understand what was going on, I would get drunk just to drown out the convicting power of God."

Night after night, James continued the vicious cycle of alcohol abuse. Feeling hopelessness and despair, he decided to put an end to his misery. After barricading himself in the house, he grabbed his gun. "I was on a suicide path," he explains. "The police were always on my back and it seemed like my whole world was caving in. I didn't know what to do, so I turned on the television and there was David Mainse talking about the Lord."

In desperation, he called the Crossroads prayer line. When one of the prayer partners answered the phone, James declared, "I've got a gun here. If you don't put David Mainse on the phone, I'm going to pull the trigger and eliminate my life!"

While the prayer partner kept James busy on the line, a Crossroads representative was immediately contacted. The pastoral counsellor soon arrived on the scene and was able to minister the love of Jesus in a time of crisis. On April 5, 1986, James relinquished his life to the Lord and became a transformed man.

God has done other miracles in his life as well. Yet one of the greatest miracles James has experienced is the power of God's love and forgiveness:

"Before my conversion, I wanted to kill those two guys who murdered my dad, but God turned my hate into love. In fact, I was given an opportunity to visit one of them who was dying of cancer. I told him that I forgave him and that the only hope for him was Jesus. We both cried like two little children that day as the Lord's presence filled the hospital room. Shortly after this incident, he also accepted Christ as his Saviour. We do serve a miracle-working God!" —KS

≈ 29 ≈

Hélène Pelletier

Winning the Game of Her Life

If the name Hélène Pelletier is familiar, you've probably been watching her as the sports broadcaster on the French TV station, TSN. Or perhaps it was that tennis match in 1985, when she and her partner won a doubles match against Martina Navratilova.

Born into a competitive family of sports lovers, Hélène began to play tennis at age 15. Practising four to five hours every day, she rose quickly through the ranks to become a Canadian champion and entered the professional tennis tour. While on tour, Hélène met a girl by the name of Wendy, who greatly impressed her. A Christian, Wendy invited her friend to accompany her to church one Sunday. Hélène complied, received the salvation message and asked Jesus into her life.

Just when her tennis star was rising astronomically, however, Hélène's personal life took a nosedive. She and the man she wanted to marry broke up, resulting in her deep depression. While she had accepted Jesus as her Saviour, she had not grown into a deep relationship with Him, and so felt a heart-wrenching emptiness with the loss of her fiancé.

Although her dream world was crumbling, the demands of the tour were relentless. The next stop was Key Biscayne in Florida – where God had a wonderful surprise waiting for her. Two dear Christian friends met her there, telling her that they knew she wasn't well. They prayed and cried with her and shared God's love.

Following prayer, Hélène composed herself and walked on the court to play a doubles match against the best of all times – Martina Navratilova – teamed up with Gigi Fernandez. At that time (1985), Martina had not lost in doubles for four years. Despite the fact that Hélène had not been able to eat or sleep, God gave her and her partner the victory in three sets. Hélène was sure it was a result of the two friends praying for her in the stands. Finally, while training in 1986, she injured the ligaments in her ankle for the 10th time, putting an end to her tennis career.

With a wealth of experience and knowledge in the field of athletics, sports broadcasting seemed an interesting alternative. With one door closing, she knocked on the next, which, following the proper schooling, opened wide for her. She is now a well-known figure at the French TSN TV station.

With her life on track, Hélène is very honest about the times when the Christian walk is a struggle. However, with her background of discipline in tennis, she recognizes the tremendous importance of discipline in living a successful Christian life – making sure that daily time is spent in Scripture reading and meditation, prayer and Christian fellowship. An understanding of the value of coaching in the life of a champion has given Hélène a special appreciation for wonderful mature Christians with whom she likes to walk. —DRL

Lord, I'm hungry for Your presence. I'm thirsty for You alone. Come and fill me with Your Holy Spirit.

❧ *30* ❧

Joseph & Claudette Pino

A Taste of Heaven on Earth

Even after 32 years of marriage, it is evident that Joseph and Claudette Pino are very much in love. However, the blissful union of this inseparable pair is actually in stark contrast to how it was several years ago....

Upon hearing the dreaded sounds of footsteps approaching the house in the night, Claudette was stricken with terror. Instinctively, she knew the faltering attempts to unlock the door were not those of a burglar, but of the man she had pledged her vows to in holy matrimony. Instead of feeling safe and secure in the presence of the one who was supposed to cherish and protect her, there was only a paralyzing fear of reliving the nightmare of violence all over again.

Concerned for the well-being of their two daughters, Claudette made up her mind to pack their belongings the following day in effort to escape the destructive cycle of alcoholism and abuse. "The next morning I turned on the TV thinking it would take my mind off what I was going to do," she remembers. "And because we didn't have cable in those days, the only program I could get clearly was *100 Huntley Street,* which I considered a Protestant program. Being raised a Catholic, I was about to switch the channel when David Mainse announced, 'This is my good friend, Father Bob MacDougall.'"

What transpired during the next few minutes was to revolutionize Claudette's concept of God, her life and even her marriage: "The first thing they talked about was how God gave His only begotten Son, and how Jesus died and paid for our sins. I remember listening to the salvation message when David all of a sudden said, 'Are you about to do something you might regret?' Father Bob then added, 'If you acknowledge you are a sinner and give Jesus a chance, He will give you peace and joy.'"

Deep within, Claudette knew that God was speaking to her. In response to the Holy Spirit's conviction of her need for forgiveness and a personal relationship with Jesus, she dropped to her knees and invited the living Saviour into her life. For two hours, she poured out her pain and pleaded to God for forgiveness and salvation. "But what do I do now?" she petitioned in prayer. "I feel hatred toward Joseph. I can't stand the smell of the booze and the effects of his drinking.... Lord, let me see him with Your eyes."

God answered her prayer. When Joseph came home that evening – drunk as usual – Claudette was no longer overcome with fear. Instead, she was filled with an intense love for him.

While reading through the pages of her Bible, she also began to incorporate the many promises of God into her prayers. As a result, the Lord began to touch Joseph's heart.

"I knew my life was not right," Joseph admits. "Then one Friday in 1978, I decided to tune to the *100 Huntley Street* telecast myself. As I watched the program, I got on my knees and cried out, 'Lord, if You are real, I want what my wife's got.' There and then, I gave my life over to Him, and to this day, it's the best thing I have ever done!"

Joseph and Claudette are now able to experience marriage as it was originally intended – a taste of heaven on earth! —KS

๛ *31* ๛

Lowell Lundstrom & Lisa

Precious Prodigal

Little did Lowell and Connie Lundstrom know, that as their beautiful little Lisa sang with the family in their great evangelistic crusades, her unresolved conflict would tear their lives apart.

As teenagers, the couple had played and sung in Lowell's rock 'n roll band. They had been regulars in the bars and dance halls in their area. In 1957, following a car crash in which they miraculously survived, they both turned their lives over to Christ.

Immediately, both enrolled in Bible college and began singing, preaching, travelling and evangelizing. Lowell Lundstrom Ministries was born and grew rapidly with their tireless attention to their calling. Radio programs, prime-time TV Christmas specials and city-wide crusades around the world were tools they used to bring hundreds of thousands of people to know Christ.

With the births of four gifted children over the first few years, the ministry team grew. The children were raised on love, Bible stories, gospel songs and prayer. To the delight of audiences, they were featured singing with their parents and playing a variety of instruments.

Somehow, in the midst of all of the ministry activities, Lowell failed to see that Lisa, his youngest daughter, was hurting. She felt sandwiched between her highly talented siblings and uncomfortable with the feeling that the crowds applauded their songs more than hers. Although she was more academically inclined than they, that was not where the rewards lay in the family. She felt that neither God nor her family cared about her. Trying to please everyone, she took every scrap of criticism to heart.

Lowell and Connie continued to tour almost every night, trying to rescue others, oblivious to the fact that their own daughter was silently drowning in their midst, a root of unresolved bitterness pulling her down.

Then came the day that Lowell got a call asking him to go down to the police station. Lisa had been arrested for propositioning a vice officer. To Lowell and Connie's horror, she had become a prostitute, working for one of the worst pimps in the business. She had decided that if she couldn't be good at being perfect, she would try to be good at being bad.

Little did Lisa understand that sin would take her farther than she wanted to go and make her stay longer than she wanted to stay.

Thus began nine years – nine painful years – of nightmare. In the midst of the agony, Lowell felt that the Lord had betrayed him. Why had God not guarded his children from Satan while he was busy harvesting souls for the kingdom? Lowell experienced what he perceived to be a triple jeopardy in his heart: 1) God had failed him, 2) Lisa had forsaken him, and 3) some of his friends were distancing themselves from him. They said that he should quit preaching and get out of the ministry, implying that no man with a daughter living such a sinful lifestyle was fit for the pulpit.

Meanwhile, Lisa, an overachiever and naturally a workaholic, began to build a network of escort services. She eventually owned seven large establishments on the east coast. Despite her determination to ignore God, the gentle, loving voice inside kept calling, "How far will you go, Lisa?"

One particularly dark day, Lowell's heart was so broken that his sorrow felt like a brick soaked in battery acid, eating away at his insides. The Holy Spirit gently asked, "Lowell, what did God do wrong that the devil went bad?"

Suddenly, a ray of hope burst through the darkness as he realized that, just as God hadn't done anything wrong, he wasn't totally responsible for Lisa's actions either. The reality of the situation came into focus and he saw how Satan had tried to destroy everyone and everything. At that moment, Lowell determined to do all he could to reach every prodigal young person within his reach. He would leave Lisa with God, trusting Him to reach his unreachable daughter.

Lowell began to view every troubled teen as someone else's "Lisa." He encouraged other parents of prodigals not to spend all of their time lamenting about their own offspring, but to get busy helping the youth in their own areas. He believed that God would honour their efforts by sending angels to reach their own families.

At the close of every meeting, Lowell asked people to pray for Lisa. Throughout the Midwest, intercessors prayed fervently that God would rescue her before she was murdered or died of ill health.

During that time, Lowell and Connie tried to build emotional bridges to Lisa by using every special occasion to send cards and gifts to her to remind her of home and her roots. As they tried to love their way back to her, God was at work and her life began to fall apart.

After nine years of sin sickness, Lisa made a call on a "customer." Little did she know that he was a serial killer who had already killed 18 girls. She was to be number 19.

The killer put a knife to Lisa's throat and stretched her out on a plastic garbage bag. Preparing to kill her, he ran knives up and down her body for several hours. Silently, Lisa cried out, "Oh, God, don't let me die like this. I don't want my family to learn it ended this way!"

Suddenly, the presence of the Holy Spirit filled the room and she felt God push back the black demon of death emanating from the crazed killer. Amazingly, the man set her free and then committed suicide.

One day, while on tour in Canada, Lowell and Connie received a call. It was Lisa. She wanted to come home. They dropped everything and headed 2,000 miles south to get her – non-stop. Forty hours later, Lisa was in their arms.

The precious prodigal was back. God had not failed. Satan had. In the years since Lisa's return, God has done amazing things. Thousands of young people have turned their lives over to Christ as a result of hearing her tell the story of her detour into darkness.

Lisa now co-hosts the *Lowell LIVE!* radio program and has appeared on *The 700 Club, 100 Huntley Street* and other national TV programs. She shares her story at women's abuse centres, homeless shelters, youth conventions, and narcotic and substance abuse groups. She is praying that her new autobiography will touch many more lives. What Satan meant for evil, God has turned into gold.

Lowell now encourages parents to take heart and not give up. From his journey to restoration, he suggests an eight-point strategy.

1. Be aware of what is happening in your children's lives individually.
2. Ask others to covenant with you in intercessory prayer.
3. Don't crucify yourself repeatedly for your mistakes.
4. Put your faith to work by helping reach youth in your area.
5. Be patient – God knows exactly how long it takes to work things out.
6. Build emotional and social bridges to your prodigal.
7. Plan a party! The father of the prodigal son told his servants to bring the fatted calf so that they could eat and be merry (Luke 15:23).
8. Keep holding on to the promises of God. Never, never give up! —DRL

Sin takes you farther and keeps you longer than you would ever expect. Money can't buy happiness – only another day of denial.

❧ 32 ❧

Frances Nunweiler

The Discovery of True Love

"It had seemed to me that the only answer was death, to put an end to all the pain and suffering." Frances was at a crisis point in her life. She had gone through enough disappointment and abuse. What she desperately needed was a caring person to be an extension of the hands of Jesus, or it would soon be too late....

Frances was brought up in Barbados in a "semi-Christian" home environment. As a teenager, she decided she was going to do her own thing, and as a result, turned quite rebellious. Her haughty independence resulted in an early marriage at age 17, and Frances soon discovered that the man she married was a homosexual.

She divorced and later married again, but found that this second man in her life had the same sexual deviance as the first. Devastated, she ended the relationship and found herself alone again.

Frances met another man and was married for the third time, hoping for happiness. Her new husband, however, turned out to be an alcoholic and cocaine addict. He was involved in many adulterous affairs and was extremely emotionally abusive to her. Despite the horrific home life she was enduring, Frances was determined to make this third marriage work, so she stuck it out... for 14 years.

Frances' heart had started to fail, adding excruciating physical pain to her long-time emotional pain. In 1992, she attempted to take her own life and nearly succeeded. Upon returning home from the hospital, her husband announced that she had three days to get out. Feeling absolutely overwhelmed, Frances called a crisis line but was told they could do nothing to help her. She threw herself to the floor and cried out to God.

Having recently started watching *100 Huntley Street*, Frances picked up the phone and dialed the number of the Crossroads Ministry Centre. That's when the miracle happened! She turned her life over to Jesus as the telephone prayer partner led her in the sinner's prayer. The prayer partner also helped her to find a local church she could attend. From that day forward, God has worked mightily in her life. Many times as a baby Christian, Frances called the 24-hour prayer lines, and someone was always there to pray with her and encourage her.

After discovering true love in her relationship with the Lord, Frances finally met her "soul mate." She is now blissfully married to a fine Christian man named Guyle Nunweiler. In addition, she has completed the telephone prayer partner training course offered by Crossroads.

In Frances' own words: "*100 Huntley Street* was like a lifeline that got me from where I was then to where I am now. I just can't express my gratitude enough for what the Lord has done for me." —RM

✍ *33* ✍

Bill Webster

Finding the Way After a Loss

As a teenager in Glasgow, Scotland, Bill Webster could never have guessed what twists and turns life had in store for him.

Having accepted Christ during a series of youth rallies in his town, he felt God calling him into the ministry. Following Bible college in Glasgow, he went to London Bible College in England and was ordained in the Baptist church. With a keen love for people, he graduated in psychology from Wilfrid Laurier University and received his Bachelor of Divinity degree from the University of London, England.

At first, life appeared predictable. Bill and his wife had two little boys, and their ministry was fulfilling. Then, in 1983, the Webster family was forever changed. Bill's wife, the mother of his two sons, died suddenly of a heart attack. Bill was devastated.

No matter how shattering his grief, however, the responsibilities of life showed no mercy in their relentless demands. His sons needed to be fed, clothed and nurtured. His home needed to be maintained. While the congregation he pastored was more than kind, the reality was that they expected him to get a grip on his own emotions as quickly as possible so that he could once more minister to their needs.

Struggling to come to terms with the loss of his wife, Bill realized that there was not much understanding of the grief process, let alone support, within the church community.

No matter how full a room might be, or how many wonderful friends he had, he was alone. Sometimes, the loneliness was so intense that it was palpable. It resided in the core of his being where its mission was the smothering of his heart. Had the comfort of the Holy Spirit not ministered healing to him, he knew that he would not have survived the pain.

As the edges of Bill's grief eventually grew less ragged, a deep compassion for others who had suffered loss welled up within him. He became aware of so many who were struggling, with little meaningful support, to keep from drowning in the grief brought by death or divorce. With this awareness in mind, he began to do some doctoral work in ministry at the University of Toronto. Uppermost in his purpose was a yearning to lead others into an understanding of Christ's ability to make every individual whole, regardless of situation.

Along with his academic work, Bill began to facilitate a program of grief support called, C.O.P.E.S. (Community of People Extending Support). In this same vein, he became the Director of the Centre for the Grief Journey and wrote several books: *Grief Journey: Finding Your Way After a Loss*; *Now What?*; and *When Someone You Care About Dies.*

Opportunity led to opportunity to reach out to those experiencing the trauma that had been allowed in his own life. Besides continuing to pastor his church, Bill became the coordinator for Singles Ministry for The Baptist Convention of Ontario and

Quebec. He also pioneered a singles camp ministry, a ministry to the bereaved, and divorce recovery programs.

From the lessons learned through his own experience, Bill now encourages others to face the memories. In the healing process, it's important not to hide from the pain, but to face it – to be realistic and encourage friends and family to share their memories.

The Lord completed Bill's own healing with the gift of a beautiful wife, Johanna, who works for the Crossroads Ministry. Her contribution to this book as researcher has been invaluable.

God's ways are not only higher than ours, but richer, sweeter, more amazing and infinitely more surprising. Only He could take the agony of lonely nights spent weeping over the loss of a loved one, heal it, and then drop it into an ocean of pain, sending ripples of compassion and healing to touch hearts far and wide.
—DRL

The only way to healing is to walk through grief, not around it.

❧ 34 ❧

Marlene Giuliano

It Is No Secret What God Can Do!

Marlene Giuliano's heart sank as she heard the tragic news of a friend's suicide. A strange feeling came over her as she thought about his involvement with the occult and the words of warning she had received from an acquaintance who was once a fortune-teller. Yet it was not enough to quench Marlene's fascination with the mysteries of occult activities such as fortune-telling, numerology, palmistry, tarot card reading and astrology (horoscopes) – in her attempt to find the meaning of life.

What initially began as an interest soon became an obsession which totally controlled her life. "I would not make a decision without checking with my fortune-teller or astrologer to find out if I was doing the right thing."

As a single woman, Marlene invested her free time into studying this phenomenon, blindly believing that it was a helpful tool. Fortunately, her involvement somewhat subsided when she became a wife and mother.

While at home raising her first child, Marlene discovered Life-Changing Television: "I found myself at home with my young son, and like many homemakers, the television became my best friend. I was led to watch *100 Huntley Street* through curiosity."

Over a period of a few years, Marlene enjoyed hearing the testimonies of program guests. When she heard the testimony of a former gang member whose life was dramatically transformed by the Lord, it really impacted her life. The Lord was already preparing her heart.

The year of her own spiritual birth came in 1978. She recalls taking her son to his babysitter, Angela, who was also a frequent viewer of *100 Huntley Street*. When Marlene confided about her marital difficulties, Angela responded, "Marlene, there is a song that goes like this: 'It is no secret what God can do. What He's done for others, He'll do for you....'"

Suddenly, Marlene's memory flashed back to her childhood. "I remember that song," she announced. "My mother listened to a radio program and that song was a part of the program!"

Shortly after this incident, Marlene listened carefully as the plan of salvation was presented on *100 Huntley Street*. "That night," she explains, "I prayed and asked the Lord to restore my marriage, and I accepted Him into my heart!"

Marlene then called the Crossroads Ministry Centre, which led to her receiving the baptism of the Holy Spirit. The prayer partner discerned her need to renounce all past occult involvement, and advised her to destroy anything that she had in affiliation with it. "I thank God for her sound advice," she adds. "It really was a turning point in my life."

Not only did the Lord set Marlene completely free from occult bondage, He also restored her marriage and brought salvation to her entire household. In addition, the Lord has opened doors for Marlene in ministry! Today she interviews high-profile personalities for a syndicated Christian radio program (JOY 1250 in Southern Ontario) and speaks at many special events and meetings.

"I'm just one little grain of sand amongst many that have formed an ocean of those blessed by *100 Huntley Street*," Marlene summarizes. "Because of my friend Angela and the ministry of Christian television, my family is saved.... It doesn't mean there are no problems in life – there are – but the Lord is always faithful!" —KS

✒ *35* ✒

/Meadowlark Lemon

"Lemon-aid" for the Thirsty

As a child, Meadowlark Lemon was always on the run. With a name like Meadowlark, it was the only way to escape the teasing! No one teases Meadowlark anymore, and those kids way back in the inner city in North Carolina wish they hadn't! Now he's affectionately known as the "Clown Prince of Basketball."

Meadowlark's no-look, wrap-around passes for easy slam dunks and his hook shots from half court are legendary. Fans in over 100 countries thrill at his ability to turn a hapless referee into a foil for his wit. They love him! Since joining the Harlem Globetrotters over four decades ago, Meadowlark has become the "hero of hard court hilarity."

As a child, Meadowlark and his friends spent Saturdays at the local cinema house, transfixed by the big screen, which brought all of their hopes and dreams to life.

One day, a film featured the Harlem Globetrotters, and for nights afterwards, young Meadowlark lay awake at night, imagining himself out there on the court – dribbling, passing, faking, jumping, slam-dunking ball after ball. The sound of the hoop reverberating in recovery echoed through his dreams, and behind it all was the sound of the crowd laughing at his quick wit and impossible moves. "Meadowlark, Meadowlark, Meadowlark, Meadowlark," they chanted. Always he had to awaken, start another day, and wait to grow up before his dreams could become reality.

God had his hand on Meadowlark from his earliest days. He remembers once falling in the path of an oncoming car, his father leaping on top of him to save his life, and the car narrowly missing them both. Memories of swimming with his friends in snake and alligator-infested ponds stir assurances that he was not alone in those days.

Meadowlark firmly believes that God gave him the relentless desire to play with the Harlem Globetrotters, and then helped him to develop his skills. Because he had no money for a basketball, he rigged a makeshift backyard hoop with an onion sack and a coat hanger. He used an empty milk can for his first two-point shot.

By the time he reached high school, Meadowlark was practising eight to twelve hours a day. Abstaining from alcohol, drugs and cigarettes, his clean living gave him stamina.

Shortly before his high school graduation, the Globetrotters contacted him. Mastering the winning combination of split second timing in both the comedic and athletic aspects of the team, his career skyrocketed.

In 1979, after 22 years as a Globetrotter, Meadowlark knew that God had given him fame and favour for a greater purpose. He became an ordained minister and began to share his love for God – and God's love for mankind.

In 1997, he celebrated his 10,000th basketball game, not only a milestone, but a world record. *The Meadowlark Lemon Show* is broadcasted internationally each week on TBN. Other outreaches include an inner city youth outreach, gang ministry, Camp Meadowlark youth outreach, youth prison work, youth drug awareness, ministry to athletes and Native Americans, as well as the promotion of health and fitness.

No group is too small or remote for Meadowlark to visit. He claims that no honour he has ever received can compare with the ultimate honour of reaching lost souls for the Lord. —DRL

God can give you the ability to do the impossible. The greater the struggle, the greater the victory!

36

Gloria Kuhn

A Life in God's Loving Hands

In sharp contrast to the light that is now shining in Gloria Kuhn's countenance is the prevailing darkness that evaded her life only years before. It was there in that deep dark pit, God reached down with His loving hands in response to her cry for help.

"I was experiencing a void in my life; an emptiness," she explains. "Everything I tried did not fill that empty spot, which just grew bigger and darker because of circumstances."

During this ten-year period, Gloria found herself facing an onslaught of crises in the family, severe and sickening physical pain, and increasing bouts of depression. In an effort to fill the emptiness and fight the depression that constantly plagued her, she pushed herself harder to achieve success and happiness. "And even though I was successful, it didn't fill that emptiness, and the depression just grew darker," she states in retrospect.

In 1990, came the darkest time of Gloria's life: "My father-in-law, mother-in-law and uncle all died that same year. By then, I was a mess. I looked awful and felt dreadful. Finally I had to quit my job – I just couldn't handle it."

Even though Gloria had never opened a Bible before nor had any understanding of Christianity, somehow she knew in her heart that there was a God. In desperation, she sought His help:

"I was lying on my bed sobbing when I cried out to God. I asked Him to take my life into His hands; I couldn't handle it any longer. Then something strange happened. Even though my eyes were closed, I saw a vision of two hands reaching out toward me. Then I had a sense of peace that I had never known before. I knew it was God. It was around this time that I started to watch *100 Huntley Street....*"

As Gloria continued her quest to discover God through Christian television, something else took place. "When I look back," she adds, "I realize that the Lord also used *100 Huntley Street* in my healing process. It would minister to me, and then I was able to sleep at night."

Eventually Gloria's symptoms of depression dissipated completely and, as a result, she no longer had to continue taking heavy doses of medication. The Word of God became her primary source of peace, comfort and healing instead.

Today Gloria is bursting with the joy of the Lord! After all, she has much to rejoice about. In '94, her husband and mother both accepted Jesus as their Saviour, and the following year her father did too! There have also been many divine appointments – opportunities to lead others to the Lord.

She concludes by saying: "Nobody knows how somebody feels inside; only God does. When I look back, I see how His hand was in everything – how He brought me through and what He has done. No wonder I want to tell the world. There are so many struggling with depression and suffering. They need to hear about Jesus and the miracles He can do in their lives too!"
—KS

✑ 37 ✑

Sharon Bryson

A Harsh Road to Wisdom

Sharon Bryson was every Christian parent's dream child. A happy little girl, she loved Jesus. Steadfast in her faith as she entered her teen years, she did not hesitate to share it with her high school friends as well as on the streets of Vancouver with her pastor dad's ministry team.

At the age of 16, however, the things of the world began to catch Sharon's eye. Rather than dealing with the ungodly thoughts as she had been taught to do, she played with them, allowing them to root in her mind.

The once happy Bryson home became filled with conflict. So unaccustomed were Sharon's parents to their daughter's rebellion that it was difficult for them to keep up with Satan's ploys. Regular marijuana use, drinking and all night partying were things they never thought they'd have to deal with – but did.

By the time she had finished her cosmetician course, Sharon was fed up with Vancouver and the authority of her parents' home. Despite the fact that they begged her not to leave, she felt that she had destroyed her family relationships and didn't need anyone anyway.

With her boyfriend in jail for dealing drugs, at the age of 17, she drove 4,000 miles to Atlanta. Smoking marijuana as she drove and stopping only twice to sleep, the trip took just four and a half days. During that time, just as she still loved God but felt too bad to be His child, she called her parents to express regret for her inability to be anything but a disgrace to them.

Once in Atlanta, Sharon again ignored the Christians who attempted to help her and involved herself with people who influenced her graduation to cocaine use. (Her father had called some Atlanta pastors he knew to advise them of the situation.)

One day, having been in Atlanta for about three months, Sharon opened the door to a strange fellow and a girl by the name of Shawna with whom she had become friends. Despite the Lord's warning within her spirit, Sharon invited them in at Shawna's request to use the telephone. By now, she had become so accustomed to ignoring the nudging of the Holy Spirit that her conscience had become seared. Suddenly, the young man slammed the door and jammed a gun in Sharon's mouth. Demanding her car keys and bank card, the two ordered her down on all fours where Shawna proceeded to tie her up while the fellow left to make sure Sharon had given them the right card code. All the while, Sharon cried out to the Lord, begging His forgiveness.

When the fellow returned, he tried to break her neck, threw her down and, with Shawna's help, attempted to beat her to death. Shawna then went to the kitchen for a knife and plunged

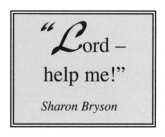

"*L*ord – help me!"

Sharon Bryson

it so deeply into the side of Sharon's neck that it grated on her backbone. In shock after having attempted to grab the knife, and cutting her hands in the process, Sharon's blood spurted everywhere. Continuing the bloody attack, Shawna plunged the knife into Sharon's stomach, face and scalp, finally leaving her to die.

Knowing that she had to live, Sharon crawled to the door, somehow pushed it open and fell on her face, her head wedged in the outside hallway in a pool of blood. As she lay, moaning and praying for rescue, Scriptures rolled through her mind. *"I am the resurrection and the life. He who believes in Me, though he may die, he shall live"* (John 11:25). Knowing that *"the wages of sin is death,"* she knew too, that *"the gift of God is eternal life through Jesus Christ our Lord"* (Romans 6:23).

In answer to her prayers, a neighbour returned early from work, found Sharon in a pool of blood and called the paramedics. Following eight hours of trauma surgery with seven surgeons, she miraculously survived a severed artery in her neck. After they had done all they could do, God restored not only the severed nerves from her face, but every deep emotional scar to the point that she does not even have nightmares.

In Sharon's words: "I believed the lie that Christianity was good for other people but not for me. I was too bad. But that's not true. The Apostle Paul himself said he was the chief of sinners. But Jesus came to save sinners. His love is so great. If I had not believed Satan's lie, none of this would have happened. If other kids trust the Lord and stay in His secret place, they will never have to go through what I did." —DRL

ᔕ 38 ᔕ

Rose Ann Makinson

Setting the Captives Free

While in an uncontrollable rage of anger, Rose Ann Makinson became terrified of her increasingly violent and abusive outbursts. Over and over again, she kept hearing a voice within her saying, "I want you to kill your kids and yourself."

In an attempt to protect her two young children from experiencing the wrath of her explosive behaviour, she locked herself in the bathroom. There, confined to the small room, she cried for freedom from the abusive tendencies that had plagued her since childhood.

Rose Ann had grown up feeling terribly insecure and unlovable. "I was looking for love, but I was afraid of being rejected," she admits. "My insecurities, along with the destructive way I dealt with relationships, only pushed people away."

At the age of 20, she started dating a friend of the family whom she had known since a child. To Rose Ann's surprise, he was very different from the rest of her short-term boyfriends. "I felt that it was just a matter of time when he would leave me like the others. It was too good to be true," she adds.

Although Keith was a wonderful husband who demonstrated extreme patience during her emotional outbursts, she still felt overwhelmingly unhappy with her life. Every effort to change her destructive behaviour only left her feeling more frustrated and hopeless. At that point, nothing – not even regular visits from a social worker – brought about any relief or permanent change.

A neighbour and friend explained to Rose Ann that she needed to be "born again." This friend also suggested that she watch

100 Huntley Street to learn more about it. "So I started watching the program daily and listened to the testimonies of the guests as they shared what Jesus had done in their lives. Although it didn't make sense, I knew in my heart that this was the way to go. I needed what these people had – love, peace and joy."

When one of the *100 Huntley Street* hosts invited viewers to

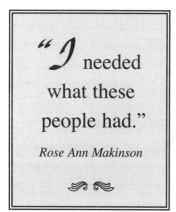

"*I* needed what these people had."

Rose Ann Makinson

call the Crossroads prayer lines, Rose Ann felt she had nothing to lose. "The prayer partner I spoke with told me how much Jesus loved me and that He had a plan and purpose for my life. That was something else I had never heard before. On that day of February 4, 1982, I accepted Jesus as my Saviour."

For the first time, Rose Ann felt truly loved and full of joy! "From the moment I accepted the Lord, I couldn't stop smiling." She laughs, "I was smiling so much, my face hurt! The change in me was so dramatic, Keith saw the difference instantly."

Within months of Rose Ann's salvation, Keith also made a decision to accept Christ. Together they began their journey through God's Word, learning about His plans for the family. Then while reading *The Bondage Breaker* by Neil Anderson, Rose Ann's eyes were opened to the real root of her destructive behaviour: ancestral involvement in the occult. "This, along with my own entanglement in the occult," she says, "explains the demonic voice I heard, telling me to kill my kids and myself."

Due to God's intervention and further ministry, Rose Ann has never again experienced a fit of uncontrollable rage. Instead, she has learned the real meaning of love. "The Lord taught me the importance of loving unconditionally because this is how He loves." —KS

❧ *39* ❧

Don Richardson

Heart Hunter to the Head Hunters

In 1962, while thousands of North American Christians sat in their comfortable pews singing, "Send the light, the blessed Gospel light, let it shine from shore to shore," 26-year-old Don Richardson and his wife Carol, a registered nurse, were carrying the light to the Sawi of Irian Jaya, a tribe of tree-house dwelling, stone-age, head-hunting cannibals.

When Don and Carol initially arrived, they knew that they risked death, but trusting God, they analyzed and learned both the language and the culture. Although both had been trained in linguistics at the University of Washington, learning Sawi was, according to Don, like assembling a TV set without a manual. Every Sawi verb could take about 40,000 forms. Learning to point with his lips rather than his finger, Don was eventually able to design an alphabet scientifically suited to the Sawi language. He then authored 19 primers and began to teach the people to read their own native tongue. Painstakingly, he translated the entire New Testament into Sawi so that they could read God's Word for themselves.

As thrilling as it was, giving the Sawi a written language and teaching them to read it was not the main goal of the Richardsons. Throughout their 15 years in Irian Jaya, their great desire was to give the Sawi people the saving, transforming message of the Gospel.

This was no easy task. The Sawi valued treachery and murder. Thus, when told the Gospel story, it was Judas the betrayer who emerged as the hero, rather than Jesus! They had been head hunters and cannibals since earliest times. "Friendship is useful," they would say, "to fatten victims for an unexpected slaughter." Of course, the Richardsons had to deal with the distinct possibility that they were simply being allowed to stay until they were adequately fattened for dinner!

Don asked God to give him the gift of wisdom in order to communicate to the Sawis their need for salvation and the provision of Jesus Christ. Amazingly, God enabled Don to resolve the cultural dilemma with an unexpectedly poignant breakthrough – the "peace child."

In every culture, God leaves a compass pointing to Himself. With the Sawi, it was the peace child. Traditionally, when warring head hunters decided to make peace with each other, a baby boy from one tribe was taken to the other tribe as a token of peace to the village.

The Sawi had been fighting with another tribe for many years. The violence was unnerving and Don finally said that unless there was an end to the fighting, he and his family would leave. They had become so valued by the Sawi by this time, that a man from the tribe ran to the enemy village carrying no weapons – just his baby son. He ran right into the centre of enemy territory and presented his child as a symbol of peace. Each villager passed by and laid hands on the child. They cried with joy and accepted him, celebrating for three days.

It was an obvious analogy of God giving his Son to the world – the ultimate Peace Child. As Don drew the parallels, the Sawi world was transformed. It was the end of head-hunting and over half of them accepted Jesus as their Lord and Saviour. Don wrote a book titled simply, *Peace Child*. It became the most widely read missionary story of all time and was condensed by *Reader's Digest* and made into an internationally distributed film. *Peace Child* was followed by *Lords of the Earth* and *Eternity in their Hearts*, as well as several others.

Having returned to North America, Don continues to work with the United States Center for World Missions, as well as the Regions Beyond Missionary Union as minister-at-large. He assists with recruiting dedicated young men and women to take the Gospel to foreign lands, as well as continuing his writing and speaking around the world. —DRL

God give me wisdom in witnessing.

❧ 40 ❧

Sarah's Story

Shelter from the Storm

It was a night a nine-year-old child cannot easily forget. Often the imprint of such trauma has been forever etched in a young impressionable mind. For Sarah, though, this was much more than just an isolated incident. It represented a series of painful memories brought on by the terror of abuse.

Reflecting back on that night, Sarah says, "I remember my parents yelling. We were used to that. But then I heard my mom scream loudly (one of her ribs had been broken). With eight children in tow – from the ages of 3 to 13 – she took us to the bus terminal. They let us go on free because we were running from an abusive situation. It was a scary night for all of us."

The aftermath of abuse did not abruptly end after arriving at the women's shelter, nor did it stop with her father's restraining order. "Even though my father wasn't in the picture, we were left with the pieces of a broken family."

At the time, young Sarah had difficulty seeing beyond the stormy clouds that overshadowed the hopeful rays of a brighter tomorrow. Then something very significant took place. On the evening of September 15, 1990, she experienced what was to be another indelible imprint on her life....

"I was 12 years old and happened to be babysitting that night," she recalls. "It was late, and all I had to do was watch TV – filling my mind with the usual garbage that is on television. When the show ended, I flicked the remote trying to find another one. I stopped when I saw this man with kind eyes. It turned out to be David Mainse of *100 Huntley Street*. I listened as he explained what it meant to be a Christian. He then asked, 'Do you want to give your life to Jesus?'

"I thought I was a Christian before, but I never knew of God's love. I experienced His love so much that night. I got on my knees in front of the TV and prayed along with David Mainse. It felt like a burden lifted off my shoulders."

For Sarah, asking Jesus into her life was the beginning of a tremendous healing process. Slowly, and ever so gently, God began to mend the broken pieces of her fragmented childhood. He also orchestrated a special friendship that was instrumental in the establishment of her new-found faith.

Being connected to caring Christians helped Sarah to grow stronger – both emotionally and spiritually. However, the situation at home was hindering the healing process. The Lord, in response to her SOS prayers, sovereignly intervened. When the youth leader and his wife opened their home to her, she discovered what it meant to be part of a healthy, Christ-centred family.

Besides providing Sarah with shelter from the storm, God began to teach her the essence of wholeness and the key to freedom from past hurts. "I knew I had to forgive my father," she states. "Maybe he hasn't changed, but that doesn't matter because I have."

As a result, this once traumatized little girl has been transformed into a young confident woman whose greatest desire is to please her Heavenly Father. "I want to do what God wills," Sarah concludes. "Because the end is so near, I can't live my life selfishly. After all, I'm not here for God to serve me, I'm here to serve Him!" —KS

∽ *41* ∾

Richard Weylman

Keys to Reaching Hard-to-Reach People

Richard Weylman is the author of *Opening Closed Doors – Keys to Reaching Hard-to-Reach People*, a book about building honest, ethical relationships.

Orphaned at the age of six, Richard lived separated from his siblings in a procession of foster homes. During those years, he attended 11 different schools, moved 19 times and was baptized into the religion of every foster home – a very negative, confusing experience, leaving him wanting absolutely nothing to do with God.

At the age of 18, discharged from the system with no money and no inheritance, he was angry and bitter, wondering, "Why me?" Having heard his grandmother say that he wouldn't amount to anything, he chose to approach life with positive determination to prove her wrong. He had already learned that negativity would do nothing but prove her right.

Emerging from a stint in the navy, Richard had learned to face the world with a cool detachment, unencumbered by emotional relationships. With a calculated eye on success, he climbed the ladder in a variety of companies, gradually reaching the top of several professions. By the age of 35, with a six-figure income, he had his own publishing business with worldwide distribution, owned a Rolls Royce dealership through which he had achieved the distinction of top sales, and travelled all over North America as a consultant. But he was totally miserable – in his words... "running out of me."

Invited by a Messianic Jewish associate to attend a "get-together" of professional businessmen, Richard initially declined. Following repeated invitations, however, he conceded that the group could prove to be a good network base for him, and so agreed to attend a meeting. This "get-together" turned out to be a Bible study. That first night, the leader taught on the house built on the rock and compared it to the unstable house built on sand, blown by every wind of circumstance (Matthew 7:26). Seeing his life reflected in the latter, Richard gradually became more intrigued. He had possessed many material things, but knew that he still had nothing.

Richard continued to attend for two years and then ventured to church. Four months later, he prayed, "Lord, if You make a difference in my life, I will serve You forever." At that moment, his whole world view changed, he was delivered of a four-pack-a-day cigarette habit and lost his taste for Scotch. Most importantly, he learned to forgive, freeing God to restore his heart.

Having experienced the entire spectrum of emotions and responses to relationships, both in business and in personal life, Richard now teaches businessmen the importance of ethical relationships with clients, contending that character and integrity are even more important than expertise. He encourages them to honestly care about the lives of customers, cultivating relationships for the sake of eternity, rather than just financial gain – claiming that business will follow. Those who have trouble sharing their faith need to understand that the first step is the development of trust and respect through an honest relationship. —DRL

I LOVE TO TELL THE STORY

Photo Album

Chris Blake (centre) and Bill Wilson (right)
with David Mainse

(Bill's story on page 170)

Joni Eareckson Tada

(Joni's story on page 150)

Nizar Shaheen with Lorna Dueck

(Nizar's story on page 182)

Joseph Tkach Jr.

(Joseph's story on page 143)

Duane Miller (right) with David Mains

(Duane's story on page 64)

Terry MacDonald-Cadieux

(Terry's story on page 166)

Deborah Klassen

(Deborah's story on page 201)

Carol Lawrence (centre) with Jenny and Chuck Borsellino

(Carol's story on page 56)

Treena and Graham Kerr with
Chuck Borsellino (left)

(their story on page 111)

Lee Ezell with Jim Cantelon

(Lee's story on page 59)

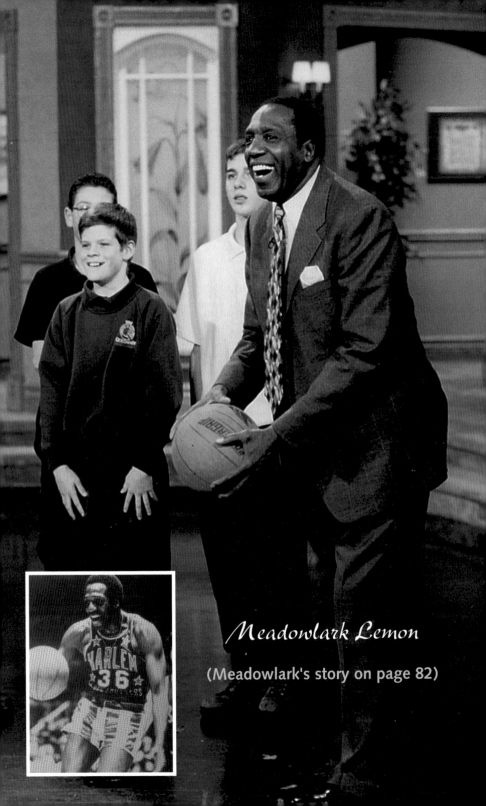

Meadowlark Lemon

(Meadowlark's story on page 82)

Georgian Banov

(Georgian's story on page 134)

*Joanne Wallace (centre) with Pam Thumb
(left) and Norma-Jean Mainse*

(Joanne's story on page 48)

Lorna Dueck with Susan Aglukark (right)

(Susan's story on page 187)

Adele Simmons

(Adele's story on page 129)

David Mainse presents Walk of
Faith stone donated in honour of
Rev. Bob Rumball (right)

(Bob's story on page 61)

Hélène Pelletier (centre) with Brian Warren
(behind camera) and David Mainse

(Hélène's testimony on page 68)

Margaret Jensen

(Margaret's story on page 99)

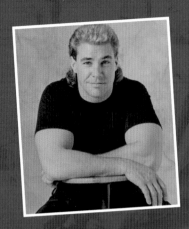

Michael Peterson

(Michael's story on page 174)

Lowell Lundstrom (right) and daughter Lisa (centre) with Chuck Borsellino

(their story on page 72)

*Bruce Marchiano (right) with
Ron and Ann Mainse*

(Bruce's story on page 208)

Build relationships. Commit your life to Christ and focus on people, not on problems.

❧ 42 ❧

Tony & Klasina Van Hees

The Fire of God

News of the upcoming event spread like wildfire in the growing southern Ontario community. It was an event that was to profoundly impact the city as a whole. What had started as a tiny spark had grown to be a major spiritual breakthrough in the lives of so many.

God heard the travailing prayers of His people. Among them was Klasina Van Hees, a woman who was gravely concerned about her husband's indifference to spiritual matters and his eternal destiny.

The rippling effect of Klasina's prayers was not only effectually at work in Tony's life, but in hers as well. When the women in her Bible study group urged her to attend a series of renewal meetings with special guest speakers such as *100 Huntley Street* host David Mainse and Father Bob McDougall, she joined them without hesitation. "The minute I got into the building," she reflects, "I was drawn by the love of the people and the music. God's presence was so strong that many were saved at every meeting."

While in that worshipful atmosphere, Klasina experienced God in a fresh new way! There was a greater sense of freedom and joy than she had ever known before, and a love for God and for others that was deeper, more meaningful than she could have ever imagined. How she yearned for Tony to know God in the same way. "Honey," he announced after hearing of her experience, "you can believe in whatever you want, but the last thing I want in this household is a fanatic!"

Undaunted by his reaction, Klasina and her Bible study group only increased their prayers for God to touch him, especially when he agreed to attend the *100 Huntley Street* rally the night of November 24, 1979.

The spiritual climate in the largely-packed auditorium was electrifying as people of all ages and backgrounds began worshipping the Lord. Tony gives his rendition of the event that revolutionized his life:

"A lot of things took place that were beyond me. David Mainse gave an invitation for anyone who wanted to commit their life to Jesus Christ. I was not capable of putting my hand up for salvation. In fact, I was making fun of those who were. I thought these people were crazy. Then the next thing I know, my hand goes up! Now that was not a voluntary action on my part, that was divine action. When I woke up the next morning, it was as if someone had put a whole new control panel inside me."

The changes were so dramatic, it astonished those who knew Tony personally. What the Lord did in those few hours would take some people many years to accomplish. And the results were not short-lived either, for they had a lasting effect on his outlook and lifestyle.

When Klasina prayed for Tony's salvation years ago, she had no idea the magnitude of her prayers. Tony now reaches people for the Lord wherever he goes. "There was a message that came very early in my Christian walk," he concludes. "Go into all the world and preach the Gospel to every creature. That message was burnt right into my heart." And the flame keeps on burning!

—KS

✌ *43* ✌

Margaret Jensen
& Jan Carlberg

Lessons that Linger

Margaret Jensen, the daughter of Norwegian immigrants, grew up eating oatmeal three times a day in Saskatoon. The family lived in a 500-square-foot home with an outhouse and a water tank, but the Lord was always thanked for His provision. Eating soup made from leftover bones, the children never knew that they were poor because they always prayed for the poor people. Many times, they wanted to give their oatmeal to the less fortunate. God always multiplied their soup and bread.

Margaret's father, a Baptist minister, filled their home with music, good books and an invaluable dose of laughter. Banjos and guitars echoed throughout their kitchen, a heady background to the aroma of bread baking in the wood stove. Throughout her growing up years, Margaret watched her mother lovingly tend the "human strays" her father brought home for their ever-present cups of coffee.

When her mother died in 1977, Margaret began to write down some of the stories to make sure that her family's legacy wasn't lost. Her daughter-in-law insisted that she send some of these to a magazine, with the happy result that the magazine wrote back asking her to "send more!"

Margaret's first story, *High Button Shoes*, was published in 1981 in *Today's Christian Woman*. In 1982, Margaret compiled some of her short stories into a collection she titled, *First We*

Have Coffee. The book was so well received that a major book club offered it as a main selection, catapulting it into the ranks of a national bestseller. Unlike many women whose worlds get smaller in their mid-60s, Margaret's was exploding with a ministry that would endear her to readers around the world as "America's favourite Christian storyteller."

> "*A*s children, we never knew we were poor because we always prayed for the poor people. Many times, we wanted to give them our oatmeal."
>
> *Margaret Jensen*

Jan Carlberg, Margaret's daughter, now a high school teacher, is thankful for her heritage of faith and humour. She attributes her solid life to the foundation provided by her parents and often ministers with her mother. Mother and daughter believe that instilling Christian values, such as those illustrated in Margaret's stories, are the key to giving secure foundations to today's children. "Thirty years ago, kids were sent to the principal's office for shooting spitballs; now they stand before a judge for rape and murder," says Jan. "We have to tell the stories, teaching about Jesus and faith in God." —DRL

Rivers of living water flow for those who are in right relationship with Jesus. Lord, I'm Yours. Make me what You want me to be.

❧ 44 ❧

Gerry Morgan

Through My Father's Eyes

The horror of sexual abuse in Gerry Morgan's life began at the age of seven. After his large family of 11 became fragmented, Gerry and his sister were victimized by the very guardians chosen for their protection and well-being.

Nudity, incest and sexual orgies were commonplace in this home, where pedophiles selfishly sought to feed their own lustful addictions at the expense of the children. For Gerry and his sister, life was a living nightmare of agonizing pain and humiliation.

Even when later adopted by loving parents, flashbacks of degrading scenes continued to haunt Gerry, causing him to react with violent outbursts of anger. At the time, his adoptive family were totally unaware of his past childhood victimization.

As a 15-year-old, he discovered a way to "temporarily" ease the pain. A trusted adult in his community introduced the use of alcohol, while taking advantage of the situation to violate him again.

"It was the first time I had ever tasted alcohol," he recounts. "What registered with me was that alcohol numbed the pain. From that point on, until the age of 30, I stayed pretty well drunk or stoned."

Emotionally, he remained a cripple – thus preventing him in early adulthood from being an attentive loving husband and father to his beautiful family. Depression and suicide attempts continued to plague him even after becoming a Christian. "One of the side effects of people who have been abused is a desire to die," he states emphatically. "I tried to kill myself a number of times."

Weary from battling the demons of the past, Gerry got on his knees and pleaded with God to take away the scars. Initially the response baffled him but now he understands. "The Lord told me He wasn't going to take away the scars. Instead, He was going to show me what to do with them."

Through a friend, he was introduced to Hans Prang (who himself came to the Lord through watching *100 Huntley Street*). Sensing the urgency of Gerry's voice over the phone and his determination to be set free from bondage, Hans began counselling him step by step to freedom and wholeness.

Gerry has experienced an incredible breakthrough in his life. Like Hans, he desires for God to use his painful past in a positive way.

As President and Chief Executive Officer of My Father's Eyes, the company that created NicoZone™ (a morally-safe Internet alternative for families), he is able to positively impact lives around the world.

What is the motivation behind his cause? "The love of Jesus," he replies. "His love through people is the only thing that cures and heals. It's the only solution!"

—KS

> ❧ ❧
>
> "*The* love of Jesus through people is the only thing that cures and heals. It's the only solution!"
>
> *Gerry Morgan*
>
> ❧ ❧

✎ *45* ✎

Pat Holt

A Finger on the Pulse of Parenting

For over 25 years, Pat Holt has been the administrator of West Valley Christian Academy in Los Angeles. With an impressive list of titles on parenting under her belt, her latest book, *Your Kids Have a Plan, Do You?* scores an "A+".

Because the majority of families is in disarray these days, parenting is in crisis. Pat has special encouragement and help for single families and grandparents involved in the process.

Sometimes, the availability of so much information on parenting can, in itself, be a discouraging factor. Who is one to believe? How does one put "what" into practise?

Working with over 450 children – and their parents and grandparents – every day, Pat has a bird's eye view of what works and what doesn't. She believes that the number one key to positive parenting is Godly consistency. If parents begin with good intentions but don't carry through with the plan, things will fall apart.

Parents need to say what they mean, and mean what they say. Those who endlessly nag simply become unheard, resented drones. The price they have to pay for inconsistency is way too high. While it may be difficult to be consistent in little things now, if they let them go, they'll reap a whirlwind later.

Consistency gets easier as parents practise it – both for them and for their children. In practising, they strengthen their "consistency muscles" and their children feel more secure knowing what to expect – whether they like it or not! While many parents have seen, experienced and read enough about the subject to know the basics, their problem is application. While they understand what needs to happen, the number one word Pat hears is "but...."

In looking at the big picture, she concluded that many parents need to be shown, step by step, how to be successful, and that is the goal of this new book. She is under no illusions with regard to the practical aspects of the job. She knows that any theory, in order to be valid, has to be able to go where the rubber meets the road. She deals with realities like inevitable power struggles, good intentions that turn to peanut butter, and personal issues that affect parenting skills.

Choices and consequences are important ingredients of Pat's approach. When children make constructive choices, there should be rewards for appropriate behaviour. Conversely, there need to be logical consequences for negative choices or inappropriate behaviour. Children need to know essentially what these will be, so that their choices will be made intelligently.

Rewards and encouragement are the best guideposts parents can give. If the children in Pat's school do well on their report cards, they are rewarded a "skip day" with a parent (an opportunity to spend some special time together as a reward). Kids want and need time together rather than things.

Children also need to know that positive choices and behaviour are honouring to God. Having a strong sense of Him being the authority over all – parents, teachers and community rules – bolsters the importance of obedience. It also gives a parent a higher court to which a child can be referred, i.e. "I'm not the one who made the rule about not lying. If you don't think it's fair, talk to God. Meanwhile, you're on dishes duty for a week."

God doesn't mind being the "heavy." —DRL

Discipline without relationship can lead to rebellion in children.

❧ 46 ❧

B.J. Raymond

Hear the Children Singing

For young ranchers, summers are truly unforgettable. Their natural curiosity toward God's creation is heightened by seemingly insignificant things, such as the sight of a tiny firefly as it moves about like a flickering spark. Equally fascinating is the warm glow surrounding the crackling campfire – a welcome way to wind down after an exciting, fun-filled day at Circle Square Ranch!

Gathered around the campfire are several children of varying ages and backgrounds – faces aglow as they sing about the wonders of an Almighty God, whose very presence is in their midst. After all, He delights in the praises of His people, and that includes His little people as well.

The ranch staff realize how crucial it is at this impressionable stage to teach them of God's love and the truth that His ultimate desire is for good and not evil, to give them hope and a future... (Jeremiah 29:11).

One such life is that of B.J. Raymond. While softly strumming the guitar, his mind goes back to his initial introduction to Circle Square Ranch. "I was nine years old the first time I attended," he recalls. "Campfire times were a highlight for me, and I looked forward to them each day. It was at campfire, I accepted the Lord."

That moment of decision was only the beginning of B.J.'s spiritual journey, for there was much more yet to be done in preparation for the bright future awaiting him. It was while working with the ranch maintenance crew at age 15, his commitment to follow Christ significantly deepened. By then, he also came to realize that he had an inclination for music.

"My mother had an old guitar in the basement which I discovered one day," he explains. "I brought it to camp thinking I would have some time on my hands to learn the instrument. Little did I know that the ranch music director was getting busier, making it more difficult for her to spend every evening at campfire. So the ranch needed a replacement, and I was the only other person with a guitar...."

These small beginnings later developed into greater opportunities. During his years in Bible college, B.J. got together with some fellow students and formed a contemporary Christian music band. News soon travelled, and so did they as the group performed in different parts of the country.

B.J.'s obedience to the will of God eventually brought about many other blessings as well – including his lovely wife Suzanne

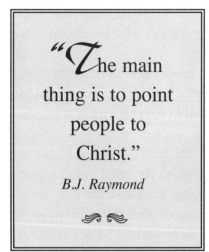

"*The* main thing is to point people to Christ."

B.J. Raymond

whom he met while playing in the band at Bible college, and a full-time position with Circle Square Ranch.

When asked about his combined ministry role as musician/songwriter and program director of the Arden ranch, he states: "The main thing is to point people to Christ."

And that is exactly what B.J. is doing as he conveys the "Good News" of Jesus to thousands of children and teens at Circle Square Ranch through his leadership and music. Heaven will no doubt be resounding with the joyful sounds of multitudes of children singing praises to God! —KS

❧ 47 ❧

Stan Telchin

Finding Jesus as Messiah!

Stan Telchin's family immigrated to Canada to escape the Cossacks in 1905. Growing up in the ghetto, from the age of five, he was taunted with the name, "Christ killer." For a little Jewish boy, it was an exceedingly painful and confusing experience.

Eventually, Stan became very successful in business. Chosen "Man of the Year" many times, the childhood taunts resonated with increasing distance in his memory. With four BMWs and a large home with a pool, Stan lived with his wife Ethel and two beautiful daughters in an upscale Jewish community – a golden ghetto. Life was good.

One Sunday evening, the phone rang. It was his eldest daughter, 21-year-old Judy, calling from Boston University. She had taken two weeks to write a letter to him; but not wanting him to read it alone and be hurt by the contents, she was calling to read it to him over the phone herself.

As she read, Stan's world shattered. Rage welled up within him, but he had no words to express its enormity. Judy was telling him that she had come to believe that Jesus was the Jewish Messiah! How could a child of his join the enemy? Thoroughly jarred, Stan then heard Judy challenge him, saying, "You're an educated man. Read the Bible for yourself. It's either true or false. Make up your own mind."

Determined to disprove Judy, Stan set about doing just that. Being thoroughly familiar with the Old Testament, he began in the New. When he got to the tenth chapter of Acts telling of the Holy Spirit falling on the Gentiles – where Peter and the apostles realized that God, not being a respecter of persons, had sent Jesus for the Gentiles as well as for the Jews – something began to click. They were saying that it was okay for the Gentiles to believe in the Jewish Messiah!

Stan was astonished! Two thousand years ago, Jesus was recognized by the Jews, but not yet by the Gentiles! How could it be that now He was Messiah to the Gentiles but not to the Jews?

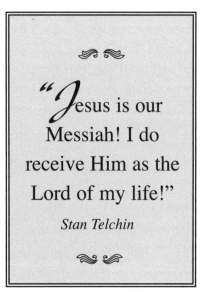

> "*J*esus is our Messiah! I do receive Him as the Lord of my life!"
>
> *Stan Telchin*

Stan became obsessed with finding truth. He devoured the Bible and discovered that Judy had been right! In the early days, Christianity was recognized as another sect of Judaism – not a separate religion!

On July 3, 1975, at 7:15 in the morning, in a burst of recognition, Stan proclaimed, "Jesus is our Messiah! He is my Messiah! I do receive Him as the Lord of my life!"

Stan's discoveries rocked his world to such a degree that he felt the Lord lead him to share his findings through writing. Thus his first book, *Betrayed!* was followed by his second, *Abandoned.*

In *Abandoned,* Stan addresses the church, wanting believers throughout the world to understand what God is doing with the Jewish people today, and how His loving arms are extended to them in a most powerful way. —DRL

We are in the end times. Love the Jewish people. Share the Gospel. Cry out to God. He is the answer.

✺ 48 ✺

Karen Gradzki

The Urgency of the Hour

Within minutes of rescuing the middle-aged man from the railroad tracks after he was hit by a train, the emergency team promptly administer the necessary medical care with utmost skill. As the seconds of time tick away, the urgency of the hour heightens dramatically – it's ultimately a matter of life and death.

For Karen Gradzki, who served in the hospital's surgical unit as a registered nurse, such emergencies presented opportune times to pray. When someone's life is hanging in delicate balance, it's time to call on a higher power. And she knows from personal experience that God is able to intervene.

"I was born with cerebral palsy," Karen explains. "The damage to the right thalamus of my brain occurred during birth. If the cell count had been lower, I would have probably been born dead. I look back from this side of God's love, knowing that it was His hand that stopped it."

Reflecting over the years, Karen can recognize the sovereignty of God in other life-threatening situations as well. However, in the midst of facing these difficulties, were the added challenges of being raised in a dysfunctional home where atheistic attitudes and excessive gambling were prevalent. As a result, Karen often struggled with feelings of being unwanted and unloved.

Thankfully, God intervened again. This time it was through a dedicated couple who reached out and ministered to neighbourhood children. This is when four-year-old Karen heard of God's great love for the first time and that He had a special plan for her life.

Although the Christian influence occurred during a brief segment of Karen's childhood, the Scriptural truths she was taught were firmly planted, despite having been raped at the age of eight by a family associate.

However, the pain of the victimization plagued Karen for years. In her teens, she sought after various forms of escape such as alcohol, drugs and promiscuity. After being temporarily satiated by these worldly coping mechanisms, she was left feeling more victimized than before.

Such futile attempts for love, acceptance and peace led her into a very destructive relationship with an abusive man. Pregnant and homeless at the age of 19, Karen had no other alternative but to give up her precious baby daughter for adoption. It broke her heart and added even more grief to an already insurmountable amount of inner pain.

Never having constructively dealt with the many traumatic events that transpired over the years, Karen's health was once again at great risk. By the time she reached 34, she was on the verge of collapse. Secular therapy proved to be ineffective at healing the deep wounds of the past. Yet God lovingly responded to her silent cry for help:

"It took place in 1991 while I was off work. *100 Huntley Street* was dealing with the issue of abuse. Through the program, God began to very gently minister His healing of the various incidents as I was ready to deal with them."

Karen is extremely grateful to the Lord for not only using *100 Huntley Street* to bring salvation and healing, but for also directing the course of her life!

The Crossroads Ministry was the catalyst that led her to a vibrant church where she later met the man of her dreams – a committed Christian who was later to be her devoted and loving husband. In addition, she has been miraculously reconciled with her long lost daughter.

And the miracles continue, for Karen has since become instrumental in the salvation of many others, including the patient who tried to end his life that day on the railroad tracks. When God leads, it pays to follow – especially when it's a matter of eternal life and death! —KS

⤷ 49 ⤶

Graham & Treena Kerr

Food for the Soul – Gourmet Style!

Graham Kerr began cooking a half century ago in the hotel owned by his parents in England. Always a very social little fellow, he was routinely shooed out of the bar, where he liked to start up conversations with the patrons, and into the kitchen, under the watchful gaze of the chef. The chef, having been taught to cook by his own father in Provençe, in the south of France, slipped some tutelage into the child care. With hilarity and priceless knowledge, he imparted his wisdom to young Graham. Where other boys were learning to dribble basketballs, Graham learned to chop, chop, chop – as fast as he could – a wonderful challenge which Graham loved.

At the age of 10, Graham fell in love with the beautiful, bubbly Treena. Following a five-year tour of duty in the army, Graham and Treena married and eventually wound up in television. With his charming, engaging personality, it was a natural environment for Graham. The "hedonist in a hurry" became *The Galloping Gourmet,* a wildly successful TV show produced by Treena.

Unfortunately, Treena was not always bubbly. Darkness had dogged her since childhood. A very angry person, she was regularly tormented with violent visions. On 60 milligrams of Valium daily, the doctor advised Graham to put her away for an undetermined length of time, as he considered her a danger to herself and to the family. Graham was devastated. Loving Treena, he had always felt vaguely responsible for her problems, but couldn't do anything to fix them.

On a particularly bad day, Treena's housekeeper, Ruthie, told her about Jesus and baptism by immersion. Always having felt the need to wash or swim after a violent episode, baptism rang a special bell for Treena. She thought it might make her a nicer person. Little did she know that Ruthie had enlisted her church to pray and fast for her for three months. She was their prayer project.

Her interest piqued with regard to baptism, Treena agreed to submit to it at Ruthie's church. The little church was jammed that night with a happy, all-black congregation waiting to see God answer their prayers. Just as she was about to be dunked in the tank of freezing cold water, Treena was thrown on her knees (by Someone). Tears began to pour from her eyes and repentance flowed from her heart as she said, "Thank You, Jesus," again and again. Having used His Name only as a swear word prior to this, her mind kept telling her that she was crazy.

Following the baptism, the pastor asked Treena if she would like to tarry. "What's Terry?" she asked, to which he smiled and explained that to "tarry" meant to wait for the Holy Ghost. As she knelt to pray, suddenly, a bright light enveloped her. She looked up and saw Jesus smiling at her. His smile seemed to erase all the bad relationships she'd had in her life.

He put His hand on her heart and then vanished. She was filled with incredible joy. Hugging all the black people, she saw Jesus in the eyes of each one. Once home, she checked the mirror to see if she could see Him in her eyes. He was there. Rushing upstairs, she excitedly told her daughter, Tessa, "I've got it!"

Not knowing how Graham would react, Treena did not tell him. However, a few days later, a woman approached him in the supermarket, saying that she had been baptized – just like his wife. Thinking she had to be wrong because Treena would probably make the water boil if she got too close to it, Graham jokingly related the story to Treena at home. Found out, she quietly told him that the woman's story was true and that she needed Jesus in her life.

With news from the amazed doctor that Treena had been miraculously healed, and having himself witnessed the return of the wife of his youth, Graham fell on his knees in an Ottawa hotel in 1974 and cried out to God. Out of his mouth came, "Jesus, I love You." He has never been the same.

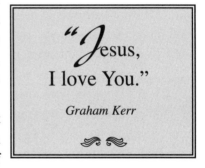

> "*Jesus,*
> I love You."
>
> *Graham Kerr*

As the self-centred, jet-set lifestyle the couple had been living during the hay days of the highly popular *Galloping Gourmet* lost its shine, they began to seek God for His leading in their lives.

With many wonderful adventures between then and now, Graham and Treena have devoted their lives to helping people achieve radiant health, so that they in turn are able to help others. One of their most recent endeavours, *The Gathering Place*, is a magnificent book extolling the warmth and fellowship shared around scrumptious home-cooked meals. —DRL

Food - Friendship - Relationship - Exercise. "Write the vision, and make it plain on tablets, that he may run who reads it" (Habakkuk 2:2).

✌ *50* ✌

Leigh & Carol Walsh

New Beginnings

Many of us would like to take a paintbrush and sweep clean some of the pages of the past. But what about God's promise to make all things brand new when we ask Jesus to be our personal Lord and Saviour? Is He really the God of "new beginnings"?

100 Huntley Street viewers, Leigh and Carol Walsh, will tell you that they themselves have experienced the miracle of new beginnings! Carol shared, "If there was one word to describe my life before I accepted Christ, it would be... MESS!"

Carol married her first husband Mike in New Brunswick at age 21. A few years later, their daughter Lori was born. Instead of happiness, Carol's life was one of emotional confusion. Not understanding how to work things out, she panicked and ran from her difficulties: "I left my first husband. He was a wonderful man, but I was very mixed up. I left my two-year-old daughter with him and moved to Ontario."

While there, Carol met Leigh Walsh. Soon they were living together, but she had no inner peace. Leigh recalls, "For over a year, Carol would cry herself to sleep. The guilt just tore her heart out. She felt it was such a terrible thing she had done and believed there was nothing she could do to make it right."

Leigh, a self-confessed agnostic, was neither interested in Christianity nor searching spiritually. However, in December of 1979, they both began to watch *100 Huntley Street* out of curiosity. Leigh became very interested in the topic of "what happens after you die," discussed with guest Dr. Maurice Rawlings (testimony on page 21).

New Year's Eve of 1980 found them celebrating quietly at home. Leigh was watching *The Johnny Carson Show* when Carol remembered *100 Huntley Street* had a special program on that evening. She suggested they change the channel.

"It was God's timing," Leigh says. "David Mainse was just giving a clear presentation of the salvation message. He talked of how our sins cause separation from God, and that through the death of Jesus on the cross and His shed blood, we can be reconciled to God and have our sins forgiven. We were compelled to call in and pray with a Crossroads prayer partner. It was the turning point in our lives!"

Carol had a longing for Christian fellowship, but it was nine months before they found their way to a home church, where they are currently involved in choir and drama productions. Three weeks after that first visit, while at a home Bible study, they prayed for the Holy Spirit to fill them according to the second chapter of Acts. Immediately after this experience with God, they felt convicted about living together and thus notified the pastor of their desire to be married.

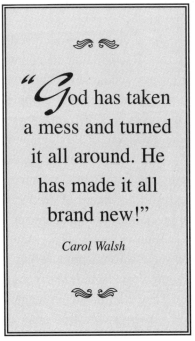

"*God* has taken a mess and turned it all around. He has made it all brand new!"

Carol Walsh

They are amazed at how the Lord has worked in the lives of their entire family – including Carol's daughter – since that New Year's Eve when they tuned to *100 Huntley Street*. "By God's grace," Carol states, "He has taken a mess and turned it all around. He has made it all brand new!" —GW

≈ 51 ≈

Ken Wales

Producer of "Christy"

Prior to his illustrious career as a film and television producer, Ken Wales was a frequent visitor in North American living rooms in a variety of television roles – one was that of Betty's boyfriend in *Father Knows Best*. Ken gave Betty her first kiss!

As a child, Ken received the Glen Ford Award for Young Actors. Recognizing his talents, Walt Disney presented him with a Disney scholarship. Thirty years after receiving his degree in film production and completing his graduate work at the University of California, Los Angeles (UCLA), Ken served as Vice President of Production for the Disney Channel.

Ken's early years as a preacher's son gave him a solid foundation in faith. It was no surprise to anyone that when he began to fulfill his dream of producing films, his projects reflected his appreciation for fine character, integrity and Christian values.

With violent TV programming having such an adverse effect on society, Ken's productions, such as *Christy, East of Eden, The Prodigal* and *Islands in the Stream*, continue to be a breath of fresh air. They offer positive role modelling with strong characters.

Christy is the true story of Catherine Marshall's mother, a school teacher struggling amid the grinding poverty of Tennessee at the turn of the century. Initially, Ken had envisioned producing it for the big screen against the majestic backdrop of the Smoky Mountains.

The more he prayed, however, the more it seemed that God was telling him to use the medium of television for it. Letting the story gradually unfold in a TV series would give a better chance to explore and understand the characters.

Still Ken resisted, intent on the vision of a glorious epic. Sensitive to his struggle, Ken's wife, Susan, reminded him of Catherine Marshall's "Prayer of Relinquishment" from her book, *Adventures in Prayer.* Catherine had written, "Our relinquishment must be the real thing, because this giving up of self-will is the hardest thing we human beings are ever called to do."

Ken knew that he had to place his dream into God's hands. After doing that, the impossible details of securing the rights and organizing the logistics fell into place. When the series first aired, it took a huge share (29 percent) of the TV audience. *Christy* was the first network prime time program where the lead character was motivated by her faith.

Ken encourages Christians to write letters to sponsors with regard to the content of programming. Viewers generally have little understanding of the weight their letters carry and the influence they have, both for and against television content. Enough letters can turn a tide. —DRL

Caregiving – the other side of mercy.

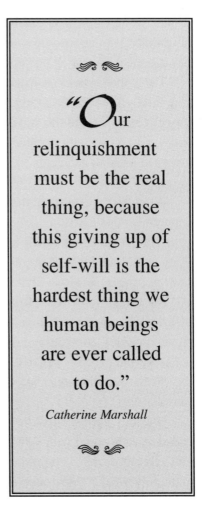

"*Our* relinquishment must be the real thing, because this giving up of self-will is the hardest thing we human beings are ever called to do."

Catherine Marshall

❧ *52* ❧

Art Francis

The Road Leading to Life

"It's urgent! We need a couple of patrol cars right away!" the dispatcher announced. Constable Art Francis quickly motioned to his partner, who nodded in agreement while gulping down the rest of his coffee. "We're on our way!" Art replied without hesitation.

The police cruiser scurried expediently around halted vehicles through the traffic to reach its destination. Within minutes, the officers arrived at the dreaded scene. The car was demolished and the driver inside indicated no signs of life. If only there was a way to prevent accidents like this from occurring, Art thought to himself.

What began as a mere thought, soon became a great prayer concern for this Christian police officer whose role as a civil servant was destined to fulfill a higher purpose. However, years prior to this incident, Art was a profound skeptic who had no faith in people, let alone faith in an invisible God.

His career in the force began in 1976. And like many fellow officers who joined him in policing one of Canada's largest metropolitan cities, combatting crime and enforcing the law in order to "serve and protect" began to take its toll. It wasn't long before the stress accumulated, affecting his health as well as his personal life.

"Besides almost breaking up my marriage," Art states, "I ended up in hospital with a duodenal ulcer, and it was pretty serious. Because my hemoglobin count was very low, I was extremely weak." This once able-bodied rookie, who aced the vigorous physical requirements of the police force, now lay help-lessly while hooked up to intravenous tubes for sustenance and medication.

"I had time to reflect," he explains. "In my silence, I began reaching out to God, confessing and telling Him how sorry I was. I more or less negotiated that if I could be released from the hospital operation-free, I would be a good guy. But after my prayers were answered, I went back to being Art Francis."

During his recovery at home, Art began watching *100 Huntley Street.* "But as a police officer, I was really cynical," he adds. "The people I generally deal with on the streets don't want to tell the truth."

Slowly the walls of cynicism that had built up over the years began to crumble. After carefully scrutinizing the presentation of the Gospel, he became more convinced of its validity. When David Mainse gave *100 Huntley Street* viewers an opportunity to receive Jesus Christ as their Lord and Saviour, Art repeated the sinner's prayer. Still a skeptic at heart, he needed more evidence to solidify his conversion.

The Lord, understanding this yearning, began to divinely lead him to unfamiliar territory. One particular day, as Art was driving home, he found himself taking a road he doesn't usually travel. While en route, he felt compelled to turn into the church parking lot. After going inside the building, something equally mind-boggling to Art took place: "One of the pastoral staff said, 'It's no coincidence that you are here.' He believed God was leading me." It was the beginning of an adventurous journey of faith and physical healing.

Art, who is presently involved with the development of accident prevention programs and a well-sought advocate on the subject, believes God has used Christian television to lead him in the right direction. It has not only changed the course of his life, but also the lives of those he is called to "serve and protect." —KS

≈ 53 ≈

Pam & Steve Johnson & Theresa

An Astounding Miracle

It was an exciting time for Pastor Steve Johnson and his wife Pam. Plans to minister in a bucolic farming community on the eastern seaboard were finally a reality.

As her six-year-old son and two-year-old daughter ate popsicles and played on the front porch, Pam happily unpacked in her new kitchen. She looked forward to the years ahead, feeling very thankful to be able to raise her family in such a safe and wholesome place.

The door opened and the little boy called, "Mom, a boy took Theresa away!" After placing a 911 emergency call, Pam and Steve searched frantically for their little daughter.

Little did anyone know that God had already alerted several of the prayer warriors, giving them a strong leading to pray for the new pastor and his children. With the church and neighbourhood mobilized to pray and search, the precious little girl's body was soon found.

Theresa had been beaten and drowned. About 30 to 40 minutes prior to its discovery, her body had been hidden under 18 inches of water in a creek culvert and weighted down with concrete blocks to keep it submerged – the realization of Pam and Steve's worst nightmare.

As Theresa was lifted out of the water, it was obvious that there was no life in her naked body. It was cold, swollen, and grey. As a registered nurse, Pam knew that she was dead. Thanking God for the two years she had been given with her little daughter, she asked the Lord for a miracle. As the Spirit of God came on her and Steve, they fought the enemy for the life of their child.

One of the members of their church, Scott Hammond, was an emergency medical technician on the scene. Disregarding Theresa's fixed eyes and the absence of a pulse, he laid hands on her and prayed. The lifeless body was turned upside down and water and sand gushed out of her mouth.

As Scott continued to pray, paramedic Jim Hansen began intense chest compressions. Inexplicably, he began to feel a warm tropical breeze blowing on his back – with no natural source. To everyone's amazement, Theresa's heart began to beat. The initial excitement was dulled, however, with the realization that there was no hope for normalcy due to extended oxygen deprivation. Within hours, the perpetrator was found and he confessed.

Theresa was airlifted to Seattle Children's Orthopedic Hospital, where she was bathed in prayer and skilled medical treatment. For six weeks, her fever raged. With a 50 percent possibility of survival, the doctors warned that if she did live, she would be horribly brain damaged.

Astonishingly, after six weeks, she woke up, obviously fully recovered. When it was discovered that there was no brain damage, the staff was astounded. The hospital magazine referred to her as "The Miracle Child." That week, the local paper carried a news article on the thousands of people praying for Theresa.

While we do not always see happy endings to the tragedies in our lives here on earth, more things are wrought through prayer than this world will ever know. As Steve Johnson says, "God can use the worst of situations in our lives. We cannot underestimate the power of prayer when tragedy strikes."

What of Theresa now? In response to Pam's prayer that her daughter would have no recollection of the trauma, God erased the memory from her mind. She is a thoroughly healthy, active young girl who daydreams at the kitchen sink, loses herself in her novels, giggles with her friends and weeps when she prays for others. The book, *Theresa – How God Orchestrated a Miracle*, details her story. —DRL

There is spiritual warfare in our lives. We must battle, but we need the help of the family of God. Many people poured their lives into this story.

✎ 54 ✎

Arnold Nogy

Let There Be Light

At first glance, Arnold Nogy's art studio looks like that of any other. But according to the multi-award-winning artist, it contains two elements crucial to his work.

The first is quickly recognized emanating from the brightly coloured TV screen opposite his easel. *100 Huntley Street,* broadcasting live daily programming from the *Crossroads Centre* several hundred miles away, carries the light of Jesus to him. The second element touches him more subtly as it quietly filters through panes of glass from the main studio window. Both of these elements are reminders of a powerful unseen Presence – the very Source of light in both the physical and spiritual realms.

In respect to his career as an artist, Arnold talks about the importance of light. "I came to the realization that it wasn't so much the subject matter necessarily, but more to do with light's affect on something," he explains. "For example, I can walk by a subject in the woods many times and not think anything of it. And then one day, when the light is just right, all of a sudden that same subject becomes interesting.... Another form of light that energizes me artistically is the light often spoken of in the Scriptures."

Long before experiencing new spiritual birth, Arnold always sensed God's presence with him. Perhaps it was because he spent much of his boyhood exploring the rugged untouched beauty of creation that he acquired an inquisitive yearning to get better acquainted with the One who so magnificently designed it all. Then one day, this wonderful Creator of light and life revealed His plan of salvation to Arnold in a different way.

At the age of 14, while home sick from school, Arnold's mother (who was on her own search for spiritual truth) routinely turned on *100 Huntley Street*. As Arnold listened to the program, God's Holy Spirit gently tugged at his heart. When the invitation was given to call the Crossroads prayer lines, he readily responded.

"I accepted Jesus Christ as my Saviour – actively putting my trust and faith in Him. I also asked the Holy Spirit to teach and disciple me, and to make my faith grow."

Not only did Arnold's faith strengthen and develop, but so did his artistic ability. Teachers began to recognize his God-given talent and encouraged him to use it in greater ways, and so did his family.

The first year he joined a local society of artists at age 17, his paintings of nature scenes and wildlife won the majority of available awards – the beginning of many that were granted to him over the years. Because of his youth, this was difficult for some of the other artists to accept. Nonetheless, personal setbacks only caused him to set his sights even higher. And his commitment to excellence proved to be worth the extra effort and sacrifice.

Among the many private and corporate commissions, his work has been honoured by the Royal Canadian Mint for a commemorative sterling silver coin collection, and one of his wildlife paintings was featured for the Ontario Fish and Wildlife Conservation print and stamp program.

"I'm so busy with commissions and my involvements with both the international Society of Animal Artists and the Algonquin Park Art Museum, I can hardly keep up! God has always been my agent. The manager that I already have in Him is the only one I need. So I can enter the picture too, being happy and blessed as I praise God and celebrate His creation!" —KS

❧ 55 ❧

Dr. Ruth Ruibal

Out of the Ashes of Martyrdom

Colombia has long been recognized as the drug capitol of the world, with the drug lords living in decadent opulence amid desperate poverty.

Julio Ruibal, dubbed "The Apostle of the Andes" by the secular press, was holding crusades with up to 100,000 people attending in the early '70s. Through Julio, God was breaking down tough walls and touching hearts in Colombia. Many were finding brand new lives through faith in Jesus. It was in those years that Julio met his wife Ruth.

Having been called to the mission field at the age of seven, Ruth was teaching in Cali, Colombia, at the university, as well as working as a consultant for the World Health Organization. With a heart for evangelism, she was also leading a small home church made up of those who she led to the Lord. In 1974, Julio and Ruth worked together establishing a church called, Ekklesia, in La Paz, Bolivia, which now serves over 20,000 people. Two years later, they married and were blessed with two daughters, Abigail and Sarah.

In 1978, at the leading of the Lord, the family moved back to Cali. With seven drug lords controlling the city, utter darkness had settled over it and there was terror in the streets. The effects of the drug cartels touched every aspect of life.

As Julio and Ruth established another church, Ekklesia Christian Colombian Centre, amid the oppression, Julio was convinced that if the people of God would gather together and pray, the enemy's grip would be broken. The problem was that there was no unity between the churches. Everyone was working independently. Julio persuaded the pastors' association that they could not afford to walk in disunity when their city was faced with such overwhelming challenges.

As the believers began to pray and intercede together, they divided the city into zones on the map and researched the recurring problems in each area in order to identify strongholds. Beginning to recognize and pray against the community's deep involvement in the occult, among other identified concerns, results began to be seen.

In 1995, the pastors called the believers together for an all night meeting of joint worship and prayer. As they prayed for God to move in their city, the mayor got on the platform and declared, "Cali belongs to Jesus Christ!" Forty-eight hours later, the newspaper headlines read, "No Homicides for the Weekend!" In a terror-ridden city where homicides were regular, daily occurrences, this was remarkable. Ten days later, the first drug lord fell. God was changing the city.

Encouraged, the church leaders rented the largest venue in the city – the 55,000-seat soccer stadium. About 60,000 believers showed up to pray and worship God all night.

As people continued to pray, the Colombian government declared all-out war on the drug cartels and six of the seven drug lords fell.

While all of this was happening, Julio and Ruth's neighbour disputed a property issue and threatened to kill Julio. Confused, Julio decided to fast and ask God what was going on. God told him that the neighbour would do him great damage, but from what he would do, the revival in Cali would spring forth.

On the way to a board meeting one afternoon, Julio's bodyguard overshot the street. Unaware of the hit men awaiting his arrival, Julio insisted on walking the block back himself. Reaching the church where the meeting was to be held, he was gunned down on the sidewalk.

As Ruth arrived almost immediately and approached Julio's body still lying in a pool of blood on the sidewalk, a great peace enveloped her. She knew she was standing on holy ground. Assured that God had allowed this for His purposes, she said, "It is well with my soul." Psalm 116:15 immediately came to her, *"Precious in the sight of the Lord is the death of His saints."*

While the press was normally too frightened to report things like the thousands of people gathered in stadiums for prayer, or the enormous crowds of believers paralyzing the city during the March for Jesus, they boldly reported Julio's murder. One secular reporter wrote, "They've killed the last living saint."

As hundreds of people gathered for the funeral, 200 pastors gathered together, hugged each other and made a covenant of unity, pledging not to allow things to divide them.

This led to a complete transformation of the city. Corruption was enormously reduced and the drug cartels were shattered. Explosive church growth began to happen – the key being unity and prayer.

Despite continued threats on their lives, Ruth and her daughters have remained committed to their call to live and minister in Cali. Ruth is now the senior pastor at Ekklesia Christian Colombian Centre. The outreach of Ekklesia includes a Christian elementary school and college, radio and television production and a health clinic. Ruth has authored many books, texts and materials for pastors and college courses. With the first 24-hour-a-day Christian TV station in the country, the effect on the people continues to grow as the necessary equipment is provided. Ruth also serves as President of the Julio C. Ruibal Foundation (a worldwide evangelistic ministry) in Largo, Florida. —DRL

God gives us the honour of giving the best we have. This gives our lives purpose and direction.

∞ 56 ∞

Kristin Draper

The Beauty of God's Grace

The news announcing that the company had to lay off 238 employees came as a shocking blow. Panic gripped Kristin Draper's heart as she tried to process all it entailed. Her income was the family's only financial source, and already their medical expenses had escalated far beyond what they could handle.

Kristin's husband Kevin, a freelance artist at the time, was having to pour much of his time and energy into the care of their young son. They had just discovered, after a series of extensive tests, that Dallas was handicapped due to a debilitating illness.

Distraught and still in a state of shock, she quickly gathered her belongings and headed home. While driving, tears streamed down her face at the hopelessness of the situation. "What are we going to do now?" she cried out in the solitary confinement of her vehicle.

Meanwhile, Kevin was busily attending to the needs of three-year-old Dallas, who rocked rhythmically back and forth in his chair. It was very difficult at times, keeping a watchful eye on Dallas' every action for hidden clues that helped them to determine his needs.

Wearily, Kevin sat down for a break and turned the channel to *100 Huntley Street,* a welcomed interruption in the midst of another challenging day. To his surprise, Kristin unexpectedly arrived home. One look at her face and instantly Kevin knew something was wrong.

"After I sat down and told him what happened," she recounts, "Kevin gave me a hug and said that everything was going to be okay. Feeling somewhat more settled, I started watching *100 Huntley Street.* The hosts, David Mainse and Lorna Dueck, were interviewing a woman who had lost hope – similar to myself. She went on to say that it was while watching *100 Huntley Street*, she realized God loved her. This testimony really spoke to me. I thought to myself, There really is a God and I know He loves me because I feel it right now."

Dallas continued to rock contentedly as they watched the rest of the program. Once again, tears streamed down Kristin's face. Kevin reassuringly responded by saying, "It's okay, Honey. Don't be sad." This time she turned toward him with a radiant smile and tearfully expressed, "Now I'm not sad, I'm happy! Thank you for watching *100 Huntley Street!*"

It was a pivotal moment in her life. And through the program, the Holy Spirit was at work in Kevin's life as well. The persistent prayers of their saved family members were being mightily answered. In fact, Kevin and Kristin were soon to discover the power of prayer themselves. "Every time we need help – every time we feel our strength waver – we ask God to help us, and He always does!" Kristen attests.

The Lord has not only supplied them with abundant provision, guidance and job opportunities, but also with an extra measure of strength and grace to raise their son Dallas, who has been diagnosed with autism. It is evident that these attentive parents consider all three of their children precious gifts from heaven above.

Between parenting responsibilities and church involvements, their lives are most fulfilling. And because of the great and mighty things God is accomplishing, they are now able to share the beauty of God's grace with others! —KS

✎ *57* ✎

Adele Simmons

No Ordinary Miracle

Out of the most intense heat comes the purest gold; from pressure and blackness, the exquisite fire of a precious gem. Out of the poverty, alcoholism and abuse of her childhood in the Okanagan Valley bush, came Adele Simmons – singing.

On good days, Adele's father was kind and funny – a Groucho Marx of the Okanagan. In those times, the walls of their home would occasionally resonate with the rich baritone of his Welsh vibrato; but having learned to drink in the army, days were not always good with him. Their home, consisting of four rooms, was regularly filled with abuse of every kind... until he tragically burned it down and the family lost everything.

Adele's mother was a survivor. She was an old-time entertainer from the barn-storming days of vaudeville. Having once shared the stage with the likes of Sophie Tucker and Johnny Weismuller, her repertoire included everything from gospel, jazz, soul, comedy, big band and country to old-time music. During her husband's stints in the army, she learned to cope alone, developing an independence that made his returns even more difficult.

The sad thing was that things hadn't always been that way. When Adele's parents were first married, they were Christians. Tragically, they got their eyes on the things of the world and fell away, preparing no foundation for their children but crumbled walls.

Fortunately, they understood the importance of sending their children to Sunday school. The people at the church soon discovered Adele's voice and encouraged her to develop her gift. With their mother's training, Adele and her sister, Jean, began singing, dancing and winning talent shows. Before long, the girls and their mother were performing all up and down the west coast.

By the time Adele was 15 years old, the unresolved effects of early abuse, hidden under the shiny façade of glamour, demanded attention. She became suicidal. Again, the church enfolded her and, at the age of 17, she accepted Jesus into her life and experienced His Holy Spirit transforming her.

Following Bible college and university, Adele added corporate management and marketing to her skills, but has continued to minister and entertain with a message wherever opportunities present themselves – in teaching, speaking, drama, musical theatre, puppetry, pageantry, variety and writing. Despite the remarkable range of her creativity, her desire to minister the love of God runs as a common thread through every outlet.

One night, two men burst into her home. Holding her at knife point, they attacked and raped her for over an hour. When she initially screamed, Adele saw the words, "I did not give you a spirit of fear," appear before her. From that moment, she knew that God was with her, no matter what. She became calm and endured the experience without getting killed in the process. Despite the fact that she was in shock for the next three months, she knew deep down that she was alright. Out of that experience came her album, *No Ordinary Miracle*, a mellow mix of sentimental and gospel music. —DRL

Learn love from the Word. God does not give a spirit of fear but of love, power, and a sound mind.

≈ 58 ≈

Richard Brochu

In Search of the Father's Love

The sounds of children happily playing outdoors are typical of a North American suburban subdivision. However, these bright-eyed youngsters are Dominican Republic street kids who have been rescued from the dangerous lure of the sex trade in their country, which relies mainly on tourism for its economy.

If it were not for missionary Richard Brochu, an ordained pastor and founder of Light To The Nations ministry, these children would be exposed to the horrors of rampant sexual abuse and child prostitution. By providing them with literacy education in a safe environment, Richard and his dedicated team are able to convey God's compassion to a community that has only known abject poverty and hopelessness. If anyone can relate to a life of darkness and despair, it is their Canadian pastor and teacher.

Born and raised in northern Quebec, Richard's father had to work extremely hard in order to provide for his large family of 10 children. As a lumberjack responsible for overseeing several hundred men, it was difficult to balance home and career. Because the work necessitated a great deal of time away, Richard remembers longing for his absentee father. His mother, who did her best under the circumstances, didn't realize until it was too late that her young preschool-aged son was the target of a child molester. To compound matters, Richard experienced further alienation and abuse at age 11 after his francophone family relocated to an English-speaking province.

"We were met with an unbelievable amount of prejudice," he explains. "All this rejection and hatred was too much to bear, and I found myself falling into rebellion. Rebellion led to many tributaries such as pornography, prostitution and promiscuity, which led to homosexuality. In this lifestyle, I travelled a great deal, always searching for love – the love of a father."

In response to the persistent prayers of a saved brother and sister, who understood the importance of spiritual warfare, God was at work: "I was just flicking the channels when I saw *100 Huntley Street*," he explains. Pastor David Mainse was interviewing an ex-homosexual who had a radiant glow on his face as he was giving his testimony. He had found the love of the Father, through God's Son Jesus. I said to myself, 'This is what I want. I'm not satisfied with my life as it is.' So I knelt down in my living room and accepted the Lord Jesus Christ as my Saviour."

From that moment of salvation 11 years ago, Richard experienced a stronger conviction of the need to break away from this lifestyle. Yet he soon discovered that the battle was not completely over.

Some members of the church he attended had a very hard time accepting an ex-homosexual into their congregation. Once again, Richard felt the searing pain of rejection. Their treatment made him want to run back to his old lifestyle. Fortunately, the Lord intervened just in time.

"On the way back to my former ways, Jesus really got hold of me and took me to a Friday night ministry where I met Pastor Angelo Del Zotto and his loving wife Carmen (see page 146). There I received compassion, mercy and grace, and really saw God's heart in action. They worked with me through deliverance as well as emotional and inner healing."

All of this proved helpful in equipping Richard for a victorious Christian life and a future in ministry within what are considered some of the most dangerous borders of the world. Many of the local people in these countries have had their lives completely turned around from prostitution, alcohol, drugs and witchcraft. As a result, an increasing number of people are being saved and set free!

"Ultimately," Richard says, "it's all about reconciling a dying world to Jesus Christ by sharing the 'Good News' and proclaiming the love of the Father." —KS

> "It's all about reconciling a dying world to Jesus Christ by sharing the 'Good News' and proclaiming the love of the Father."
>
> *Richard Brochu*

✎ 59 ✎

Georgian & Winnie Banov

The Sound of Freedom

Wrapped in the steely cold secularism of Communist Bulgaria, Georgian Banov's musical gifts emerged in early childhood. At the age of five, he began to train as a classical violinist and played in symphony orchestras throughout junior high.

But those were the early '60s and Georgian was not so insulated from the world that his veins did not fill with the rock 'n roll passion of his international peers. Forming the first official rock band in Bulgaria, for which he was drummer and lead singer, he led the youth in a revolt against the Bulgarian establishment. Disbanded by the government, he continued to study percussion, flute and piano in a Bulgarian college.

Seeking freedom, Georgian and his guitar player escaped, smuggled by a black market dealer, out of the country in the back of a cab. Emigrating to the United States, Georgian sought fame and fortune in Hollywood, but found only disappointment.

What he did find, however, was a group of street-witnessing Christians who broke through the cold walls of his heart with the message of the Gospel. Initially, their freedom and joy made him wonder what drug they were on. However, challenged with the possibility of the actual existence of God, he went up on a high hill where Jesus met him in a powerful way. Accepting Him as his personal Lord and Saviour, Georgian finally found freedom, not just externally, but internally. No longer was he oppressed by the heavy blackness of secularism and atheism.

Meanwhile, the girl who would one day be his wife, Winnie, was seeking truth in India. Disappointed when she discovered that the gurus didn't have it, she returned to the United States to stay with her sister, a Christian who had been praying for her. When she finally found Jesus – the embodiment of truth – she spent hours with God, soaking up His wonderful love for her and seeking His will for her life.

When Georgian met Winnie, he was impressed with her dedication to God and knew that they could grow in ministry together. They married and had a daughter, Yana.

Moving to Texas, Georgian studied and was ordained as a minister of the Gospel. In 1980, he and his co-producers formed *Silverwind*, an enormously successful contemporary Christian music group. Finally, the pieces of his life were coming together in God's perfect design. His carefully honed musical skills, coupled with his new-found spiritual gifts, were invested into the spreading of the Gospel.

With songs on three successful *Silverwind* albums and such popular children's records as *Bullfrogs and Butterflies* and *Music Machine* (both gold albums), Georgian's song writing skills became recognized throughout the world. But something still wasn't right.

Georgian and Winnie began to fall away from their early passion for God. They had tried too hard and given too much without resting and receiving God's love. A mission trip to poverty-stricken, war-torn Uganda left an indelible impression on Georgian that resulted in major changes in his ministry. After 12 years of Christian service and "works" for God, he discovered His grace and love in a brand new way.

Founding *Celebration Band International*, as an outreach devoted to continuing the work begun in Uganda, he went on to complete a family album, *Papa's Rainbow*, an allegorical musical on the promises of God to His children.

Georgian and Winnie now tour throughout North America conducting powerful times of ministry with their anointed music, powerful testimony, messages of encouragement and proclamation of who we are in Christ. With the Iron Curtain having gone to the cleaners, he has also been taking Bibles to Bulgaria and preaching the Word to his homeland. —DRL

It's important to know how to <u>receive</u>, not just how to <u>do</u>. Don't get swayed by religion, away from relationship.

❧ 60 ❧

Wilf & Marguerite Kalina

God's Fishing Pole

Marguerite Kalina crept into the kitchen of their motor home to get the biggest knife she could find. After another night of drinking and fighting with her husband Wilf, she slid into a slimy pit of despair. To Marguerite, murder-suicide seemed the only way to end the misery.

Surprisingly, Wilf and Marguerite came from very similar backgrounds. They were both born in Germany during the year 1937; and because of unfortunate circumstances, both were raised by their grandparents. Married at only 19 years of age, the young couple had no choice but to live in one room at Wilf's grandparents' small home. The situation became even more uncomfortable after the birth of their first child. At that point, Wilf's mom moved in with them. It was not a good scene.

Wilf and Marguerite longed to escape the constant strife within the family, and thought that immigrating to Canada would solve their problems. They arrived, only to discover that Wilf's mom had secretly immigrated and was awaiting them!

The Kalinas easily slipped into the party scene to escape facing real issues, and the family feuds accelerated as did their heavy drinking. Wilf says in retrospect, "There was a downturn in the building industry and our escape from this stress was even more drinking. I didn't know where else to turn." Eventually, they lost their home and construction business.

Marguerite searched in the occult for answers. Then one memorable day in 1983, she turned on a program called *100 Huntley Street.* "It was God's fishing pole drawing me in," she explains. "I kept watching on and off with alcoholic drinks in my hand – just weeping. Oh, how I longed to know God like these people. I got hooked!"

The Kalina's had begun attending a nearby church in an attempt to get their marriage back together, but at an outing with friends, alcohol again fuelled a fight. "This was the night all hell broke loose," Marguerite says in reference to the destructive work of the enemy. The situation got so bad, she decided to end it all.

Then something most unusual took place. Suddenly a vision appeared before her and she heard the voice of David Mainse saying, "Don't take your life... give it to Jesus Christ." Meaning it with all of her heart, she responded, "Well, I don't really think He wants it; but if He does, I give it to Him now."

When Marguerite awoke the next morning, everything was different! God had not only delivered her from alcohol, but from blaming others. Instead of feeling angry, she had a compelling desire to go and hug Wilf! Sober now, Wilf happily responded, sorry for his actions too.

Not many days later, driving home in his truck, Wilf cried out to the Lord, "You have bigger shoulders than I do, God. Take this burden from me." A peace – like liquid love – flowed over him. His desire for alcohol was gone. "God delivered me when I really meant it, and our lives have never been the same!"

The rest of the family could not believe the transformation. One by one, they came to know the risen Lord for themselves – including Wilf's mother who has since gone on to heaven!

Wilf and Marguerite's lives are now consumed in worthwhile ways – to know the Lord more and to make Him known to others. "We can't keep the good news to ourselves!" Marguerite concludes. "If we can encourage people to watch *100 Huntley Street*, we know it will change their lives – like it did ours – and start them on their spiritual journey. It's God's fishing pole!"

—GW

≈ *61* ≈

Stephen Saint

Lessons in Courage

Sometimes the symbolism of a person's name is striking. This is one of those times. Stephen is a "Saint" with family connections in parallel worlds.

In 1956, Steve's father, Nate Saint, was a missionary pilot serving in Ecuador's Amazon rainforest at the beginning of the outreach to the Aucas (now known as the Huaorani Indians). After making the initial contact with the stone age tribe, Nate and four other missionaries attempted to meet them again with the purpose of sharing the Gospel.

Tragically, their purpose was misunderstood and the Indians, in a very bad mood that day, set a trap for them. At a moment when the missionaries were distracted, they were ambushed by a group of warriors who attacked with spears. Nate and the others were faced with the choice of either killing or being killed. They chose only to fire their guns into the air and so died that day, speared to death.

Days later, their bodies were found floating in the jungle river in mute testimony to their love for the Huaorani. While the story made headlines around the world, the greater story followed. Nate's wife Marjorie, with her three children (including Stephen), went to live in Quito. Stephen's aunt, Rachel Saint, along with the wife and little daughter of Jim Elliot (another of the martyrs) returned to the jungle.

Invited by the tribe, Rachel, knowing that there were no roads, no mail and no hydro, stayed to live and work with the Indians. Often during school vacations and summer holidays, Stephen would stay with his aunt. Thus he grew up knowing the Huaorani.

While raised with a deep understanding of the great importance of getting the message of Jesus to the Indians, Stephen missed his father and harboured a gnawing sense of his having died needlessly.

One day, stranded in Timbuktu – at the end of the earth – Stephen had a very strange adventure. He happened on a young Christian man, Nouh Ag Infa Yatara, and a missionary, Mr. Marshall. Having responded to Mr. Marshall's message as a child, Nouh had been disowned by his family for the shame his belief in the Bible brought to them. Their attempts to poison him having failed, they recognized God's intervention in his life and so allowed him to live, condemned as an outcast.

Curious, Stephen asked Nouh where his courage came from – courage that enabled this teenager to take a stand for his faith, making him despised by the whole community. His eyes widened as Nouh told him about reading a story of five young missionaries who willingly risked their lives to take God's

"Good News" to stone-age Indians in the jungles of South America. Nouh continued, "The book said these men let themselves be speared to death, even though they had guns and could have killed their attackers!"

Mr. Marshall looked at Stephen. "I remember the story. As a matter of fact, one of those men had your last name.

"Yes," Stephen said quietly. "The pilot was my father."

Following an afternoon of further sharing, with parting hugs, the two young men left priceless gifts for each other: Stephen gave the assurance that the story which had given Nouh courage was true, while Nouh gave Stephen the assurance that God had used his father's death for good. By dying, Nate Saint had helped give Nouh a faith worth *dying* for. Nouh, in return, helped give Nate's faith back to his son – a faith worth *living* for.

When Stephen's aunt Rachel finally died in 1994, after many years of missionary work in the Amazon, Stephen was asked to return there to bury her. When the Indians told him he needed to go to be with them, after much prayer, he did. Living with the very men who viciously killed his father, in the love, peace and reconciliation that only Jesus can bring, he moved with his family into a new "clearing" and lived as they lived for about one and a half years. So deep has been the healing, that Mincaye, one of the killers, is a "grandfather" to the Saint children and has travelled with Stephen as a missionary from the tribe, sharing his testimony across the United States and Canada as well as to Amsterdam 2000. Can there be a greater story of forgiveness and love through the grace and redemption of Christ?

Stephen now maintains his home in Florida, and returns to the jungle village several times a year. —DRL

We're all giving our lives to something. Live a life that counts and do it now.

⤳ *62* ⤳

Ruby & Lorne Hoisington

God's Healing Touch

Walking hand in hand, Ruby and Lorne Hoisington can at last enjoy the simple things in life that many of us take for granted – the sights and sounds of nature, the vibrancy of life and good health.

At one time, however, they weren't able to share such wonderful moments together. "I was probably in the hospital about 18 times due to back pain," Ruby recollects. And despite many years of medical help, the pain eventually progressed to the point of paralyzing her. She was then confined to her bed or the living room chesterfield.

Every morning, Lorne routinely carried Ruby into the living room, where she lay all day on the chesterfield. It became a regular way of life. Those were difficult years for both Ruby and her family as she was unable to care for them.

Years later, God began working in her heart. "I don't know if it was by accident, but my daughter Lorna turned on this program," Ruby continues. "I was really drawn to what I was hearing. Such soft voices... I heard them mention that it was *100 Huntley Street.*"

One day her son Terry rushed out of the door to get to school on time. Lying on the chesterfield, she realized he had forgotten to turn the channel for her usual TV show.

"*100 Huntley Street* came on instead, the same program I had watched once before," she adds. "The program guest, Mary Goddard, had a word of knowledge: 'There is a woman laying on a chesterfield with a chronic back condition who isn't able to move. Right at this very moment the Lord is healing her.' I had never heard of anything like this before, and yet while she was talking, my back felt like it was on fire."

While experiencing God's tremendous healing power, Ruby heard someone on the program say, "Try and do something that you have never been able to do before." Slowly she manoeuvred herself into a sitting position. There was no pain. Then she swung her legs around and touched the floor, and still felt no

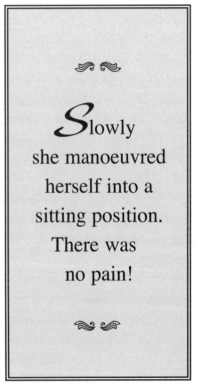

*S*lowly she manoeuvred herself into a sitting position. There was no pain!

pain! When she got on her feet, she started walking around slowly. Soon Ruby began running all over the house. "I ran up and down the stairs," she exclaims, "I hadn't been up and down those stairs for so long. It was glorious!"

Ruby certainly has much to rejoice about, especially considering the fact that almost all of her family members have come to know the Lord Jesus as their Saviour! And nothing is stopping her from enjoying the vibrancy of life either. In fact, she is making up for all those years of confinement by walking, swimming, bike-riding, drama, singing in the church choir and even line-dancing!

"To see my mom now is like a gift," Lorna sums. "It's great to watch her enjoy the grandkids. She can pick them up and swing them around, and do all the things that she wasn't able to do with us. There's just no describing it!" —KS

✤ *63* ✤

Joseph Tkach Jr.

Transformed by Truth

Following the death of Herbert W. Armstrong, founder of the Worldwide Church of God, Joseph Tkach Sr. became the Pastor General and Chief Administrative Officer, as well as President of Plain Truth Ministries. Since the mid '60s, under his leadership, the Worldwide Church of God has undergone a radical transformation from the old teachings of H.W. Armstrong.

Prior to his death in 1995, he appointed his son, Joseph Tkach Jr. as his successor. Joseph Jr. has served the church as an ordained minister since 1976. As he has continued his father's work, the church has been transformed by truth. Since the late '70s, the Holy Spirit has blessed the group with unprecedented growth in doctrinal understanding and sensitivity to the world around them, resulting in monumental, historic reforms.

Gone is the legalistic interpretation of the Old Testament, which H.W. Armstrong used to interpret the New Testament, rather than interpreting the Old in light of the New, as God intended. In its place is the New Testament's central theme: the life, death and resurrection of the Lord Jesus Christ. Now salvation is recognized as a work of grace, based on faith alone.

Gone is the old belief in British Israelism and insistence on the fellowship's exclusive relationship with God. Gone are the condemnations of medical science, the banning of the use of cosmetics, and the rejection of traditional Christian celebrations such as Easter and Christmas.

God is now recognized as existing eternally as three Persons, known as the Trinity: the Father, the Son and the Holy Spirit. No longer is He viewed as a "family" of multiple "spirit-beings" into which humans may be born.

Where people were once encouraged to pray privately rather than in groups, the church now has close to 2,000 small prayer groups. Since this remarkable turnaround, Joseph Tkach has embraced other Christians, apologizing in *Plain Truth* for calling them, "children of the devil."

The cost, however, has been great. One member actually wanted Joseph publicly executed for challenging H.W. Armstrong's traditional beliefs. One third of the pastors opposed him and the denomination split, with a loss of half of the membership.

How glorious it is that those who remain finally have "the plain truth." —DRL

It's important to forget the fear of other people and get to know Jesus.

≈ 64 ≈

Agostino Molinaro

Delivered From Destruction

"Your son will either die within two hours or he will be a vegetable for the rest of his life." Those were the shattering words spoken by the neurologist to the parents of Agostino Molinaro after performing brain surgery for 12 hours on their son. For the next three and a half months, they anxiously awaited for signs of life as he lay in a coma.

When 24-year-old Agostino finally awoke in the unfamiliar surroundings of the hospital room, he recollected the series of events that took place that almost fateful day....

It took place the morning of March 7, 1978. The rock music played in the car as Agostino drove to an isolated area after a party. He had tried it all – drugs, sex and "partying" – yet loneliness and depression continued to overwhelm him. Tired of searching for meaning and acceptance, he held a gun to his head. Due to a reflex reaction after the first shot, a second one went off immediately after – both bullets penetrating the right side of his brain.

The resulting brain damage caused excruciating pain throughout his body. Agostino also faced the gripping reality that he could not move or even talk. "When I woke up from the coma, I couldn't speak.... I knew what I wanted to say, but I couldn't get the words out."

Besides having to deal with the inability of expressing himself verbally, Agostino felt frustrated with the limitations of life in a wheelchair. After overhearing some nurses discussing his condition, someone finally concluded: "Agostino will never be able to walk again." These words were like a death sentence, echoing in his mind over and over again as he sat in the wheelchair and stared out the window.

During this time of discouragement, Crossroads prayer partner Ruth Rose prayed for him during one of her visits to the hospital. As she went on her way, Agostino prayed, "Oh, God, if this woman said the truth about You and if You're real, then please get me out of this place. I want to tell people about You." God heard his prayer.

Soon he was transferred to a rehabilitation centre for nine months of therapy to relearn basic skills and speech. While turning the dial of his roommate's TV, he came across *Vivere al Cento per Cento*, an Italian Christian program produced by

Onofrio Miccolis at the Crossroads Centre. Agostino carefully listened as Onofrio, along with daughter Esther, shared more about the reality of Jesus. His heart was so moved that he responded to the invitation to call the phone number on the program for prayer.

Over the years, Agostino has become a new man – totally delivered from a destructive past and given a future of exciting possibilities! And now that he can walk with the assistance of a cane, his daily prayer has become, "Lord, please guide me where I'm to go."

Agostino has not only been divinely led to work at the Crossroads Centre as a prayer partner, but also as far as the Dominican Republic, Italy and Israel in order to tell others about Jesus – the One described in Psalm 107:20 who is able to *"deliver them from their destructions."* —KS

✺ 65 ✺

Dr. Angelo & Carmen Del Zotto

Believing Jesus

Angelo Del Zotto is a genuine Italian "papa." A tall, well-built man with little need for a brush and a physique that hints at his love for Carmen's spaghetti, he has a hug that can strengthen the most wounded heart. Usually beside him is Carmen, a trim, beautifully groomed Italian lady, with a very strong, yet gentle demeanor.

For years, Angelo worked in management in the insurance industry. He and Carmen had been born and bred in the traditions of their church and felt they needed nothing more spiritually.

In the early '70s, Carmen's sister, Rose Simone, one of the first counsellors at *100 Huntley Street*, annoyed Angelo and Carmen to no end with invitations to her Thursday night prayer meeting where she claimed that something new was happening with the Holy Spirit – that His joy was available to them.

Following surgery, unable to get to the remote to change the channel, Angelo began to watch some Christian television. There, he saw people just like him, with all of the same struggles and challenges he faced, but with a difference. They were so happy! Finally, one night, both Angelo and Carmen decided to let go of their traditional beliefs and allow Jesus to reveal Himself to them in His own way. They committed themselves to Him, and life has never been the same.

Immediately, they began to relax and found such love bubbling inside that they wanted to embrace the whole world. One of their six children brought home a boy who had been living in a car – and he simply stayed as one of their own. On Sundays, their home would be filled with 50 or 60 teenagers who wanted to hear about the Lord. Carmen and Angelo would feed them a lot of spaghetti with a good measure of the Word and today, many of those young people are pastors, missionaries and backbones of local churches.

Gradually, with more and more people seeking them out for counsel, Angelo became accredited with the Pentecostal Assemblies of Canada (PAOC) and began to pastor in a Toronto church. Writing a book with Diane Roblin Lee, *Developing Intimacy in Marriage*, he and Carmen began to give relationship seminars across the country.

The thing about Angelo and Carmen was that they really believed the Bible. When they prayed, they expected to see

God's answers and so they did. Amazing things began to happen that they simply took for granted. People were healed, delivered and restored from all kinds of incredible circumstances (testimony of Richard Brochu, page 131).

Astounded at the lack of understanding people had about the reality of spiritual warfare, Angelo began another book with Diane, *Freedom from Darkness*, now one of the most powerful and practical books available on the subject. Through it, Angelo demystified deliverance. With reassurance that a Christian cannot be demon-possessed, he warns that they can be demonized, or harassed by demons which prey on areas of weakness. *Recognition* of areas of weakness, *repentance* of sin and *rejoicing* in the freeing power of Jesus will result in freedom.

In 1995, Angelo and Carmen were required to walk through deep waters following Angelo's diagnosis with lymphoma. With the cancer raging through his spleen, his liver, and virtually his entire body, he progressed into the final stages. All who love him were horrified to see his weight quickly drop to almost half of what it had been. With people praying across the country – and despite the fact that he and Carmen stood on the Word, took authority over the disease and trusted God to see them through – nothing seemed to change. It wasn't until Angelo recognized the resentment in his heart towards someone, requested forgiveness and then defended the person publicly, that his terribly emaciated body began to respond once more to life. Fully healed, he went on in his studies and received his doctorate.

Today, Angelo and Carmen's single desire is to give God the glory for all that He has done and continues to do through them in the lives of others. —DRL

The body of Christ (believers) is so important in times of need. We must take on the mantle of forgiveness.

≈ 66 ≈

Mary Lindsay

The Missing Key to Her Heart

A few hours earlier, Mary Lindsay, a volunteer at a prison, had felt reluctant to spend the evening at the correctional institution located in her city. Now as she drives home after both chapel services, thoughts of how God moved in the hearts of the inmates fill her with great joy.

Every week, Mary participates in the two Sunday evening services and one-to-one counselling provided for male offenders. As the weeks progress, she senses a tremendous spiritual hunger and openness to the Gospel amongst many of these once hardened criminals. After all, nothing is impossible with God.

This truth became real to Mary personally during a time of loneliness and heartbreak, due to the devastation of divorce. Resentment, unforgiveness and anger consumed her. She admits, "All this was destroying me – pulling me down. I couldn't even function properly. My minister and friends kept telling me to forgive, but I just couldn't do it."

Mary knew she needed help, so she decided to take a friend's advice and watch *100 Huntley Street*. "The more I got interested, the more I watched," she says. "I could see that people's lives were being changed... people's needs were being met."

When David Mainse interviewed a guest on *100 Huntley Street* who was in the same predicament, Mary listened thoughtfully to his testimony. She recalls, "Even though he knew he had to forgive, he could not do it in his own power. So he prayed that Jesus would help him."

At the end of the program, David invited the viewers to receive Jesus as Saviour by saying, "Ask Him to come into your heart and you will find the peace and forgiveness you are looking for."

Finally, Mary found the missing key to the door of her searching heart. "I had gone to church all my life and thought I was a Christian," she confesses. Yet it was that day while watching *100 Huntley Street* she first realized her need for Christ as Lord and Saviour.

"It's indescribable!" she adds. "Like the song that Norma-Jean sings, 'He changes us from the inside out.' All the things that we can't do for ourselves, He can do!" —KS

≫ 67 ≈

Joni Eareckson Tada

Wow!

One of those gorgeous, all-American girls who just "had it all" – brains, personality, athletic ability and a great family – Joni spends her days in a wheelchair.

Diving in the Chesapeake Bay one golden July day, she broke her neck. But God had a plan. He would enable the teenager, just voted by her high school class of '67 as "the most outstanding girl," to prove her classmates more than right, in ways they could never have imagined.

Paralyzed from the neck down, Joni's life could have been spent gazing longingly at the world from behind a gauze curtain – but it isn't. Following two years in rehabilitation, Joni became an internationally known mouth artist; the founder and president of JAF Ministries (an organization that ministers to disabled people); the author of over 20 books; radio show host on the five-minute daily, *Joni and Friends*; a columnist for the *Moody Monthly*; board member for such concerns as the Lausanne Committee for World Evangelism; advisor for the American Leprosy Mission, the National Institute for Learning Disabilities, Love and Action, Youth for Christ International and the Christian Blind Mission – much more than most able-bodied people ever envision accomplishing.

Where others might have chosen to wallow in justified self-pity, Joni collects wheelchairs for the handicapped community around the world, records her songs, inspires groups across the country and enjoys marriage to Ken Tada, the wonderful husband God gave her.

But why settle for life in a wheelchair, when God not only calls Himself our Healer, but has proven Himself over and over and over again in healing others? After seeking healing for many years, that's a question that has finally been settled in Joni's mind. When in Jerusalem in 1998, she cried out to God once again at the Pool of Bethesda. As God's peace filled her, she realized that He had already healed everything that needed healing in her life. The wheelchair was a gift, giving her a voice for His love that she would never have had without it. Because God always seems bigger to those who need Him most, she proclaims His love more loudly than she would have without it. It makes a powerful difference in her life, causing her to lean on God in her weakness and need, to know Him with a depth that would have been otherwise impossible.

In these days of considerations of euthanasia and diminished value of life, Joni claims that we live in a culture of death, where the value of a human is based on acceptability and ability. *When God Weeps* articulates our lack of understanding of life and suffering. In it, Joni demonstrates why the "right to die" is no favour to the disabled who can bring a special gift to the world even through pain or disability.

Despite the fact that Joni knows from experience how God permits suffering to wake us from our spiritual slumber, she has never become accustomed to her wheelchair. It is new to her every morning, causing her to cry out to God daily.

Having always been a great friend to others, Joni has reaped the rewards of steadfast friendship. At 7:30 every morning, girl friends arrive to get her ready for the day. Off to her office at Joni & Friends in southern California, once again, she makes her life count to the glory of God. —DRL

The weaker I am, the harder I lean on Jesus. God seems bigger to those who need Him most.

≈ 68 ≈

Ralph (Groat) Richards

A New Song

Sounds of laughter fill the large auditorium as hundreds of seniors enjoy the jokes of entertainer and musician Ralph Groat (known professionally as Ralph Richards). Even at 73 years young, he performs all across the country. He is thankful for having these opportunities to be a bold witness through music – especially in audiences such as this, where there are many who do not yet know the Lord Jesus Christ as their personal Saviour.

Ralph's love for music began in childhood, while listening to his mother play the piano. Later known by her church family as "Grandma Groat," she faithfully served as church pianist for 43 years. During those years, Ralph could never fully understand the reason for his mother's constant joy and contentment. It was not until five years after her death and some heart-wrenching circumstances in his own life, that he finally realized all his success in the entertainment business meant nothing at all.

Having a reputation of dependability, along with the ability to write and perform lively piano music, Ralph has travelled nationally for the past 50 years. His career included performing publically, as well as in commercials and various television and radio programs. Life was very exciting in those early days, yet it proved to be very demanding for him as a husband and father. And like many in the entertainment world who are too busy achieving success, Ralph also admits, "There was no time for God; no time for anything spiritual."

As a result of some extremely stressful circumstances in his professional and personal life, Ralph found himself heading toward a breaking point. He explains, "My stress level was like a pressure cooker ready to explode." Not only was this time in Ralph's life a breaking point, but also a turning point. Desperate for help, he began watching *100 Huntley Street*. When he heard the testimonies on the program, something tugged at his heart, and for the first time in years he began to reflect on the evangelistic camp meetings he attended with his mother as a child. Then the Lord began to gently speak to him. Ralph recalls this life-changing moment:

"Deep within, the Holy Spirit said, 'Ralph, it's time you made a decision for the Lord.' It was January 1, 1979. I knelt down beside my bed and prayed a very halting prayer. I only got as far as a word I hadn't said in 40 years – the precious Name of 'Jesus.' Then the Holy Spirit ministered to me in a very dramatic way."

Four months later, on May 22, the Holy Spirit also completely healed him from a lifetime of headaches. "That was over 22 years ago," he explains, "and I still have no headaches."

Thankful for all the Lord has done, Ralph says, "I honestly don't know how I got by without Jesus before. Even though I went through some real turmoil after becoming a Christian – at times my life was anything but smooth – through it all, I had that inner peace that only He can provide." —KS

⋟ 69 ⋞

David Nash

The Gift of Life – Through Death

"David, in order for you to live, someone will have to die." As a pastor who had dedicated his life to caring for others in their need, it was difficult for David Nash to process the thought of benefitting from someone else's tragedy.

David had grown up in a Nazarene parsonage, the product of generations who loved and served God. As a child, his grandmother, who lived with the family, would pay the children to memorize Scripture. The call to his own ministry came when David, a six-foot-six redhead, was a junior in high school. He never veered from his course.

David loved people. Having become ordained, and served congregations in Pennsylvania, Tennessee and Illinois, he was now ministering in Chicago. He visited the sick, stood by people when their loved ones died, and generally, loved his life. God was great, life was full and the future was bright – until now. Having prayed many times for others to be healed, he now prayed fervently for himself. David would die without a new liver.

In a time of personal need, all kinds of wild thoughts try to thrust themselves into the confusion of fear. Despite the fact that he had committed his life to Christ and knew that God had called him into ministry, David endured thoughts of God not caring for him or having left him.

But God is faithful and has promised never to leave us nor forsake us. Any negative worries to the contrary only point to increased evidence of His steadfast love for His children when His hand is revealed. His timing is impeccable.

In another town, a 37-year-old man named Serafino went to work. While screwing in a light bulb, he fell and died, shattering the dreams his wife Sonni had for their loving future together. Devastated, she determined to retain as much of his life as she could by donating five of his organs.

Many in David's life wrote to Sonni to thank her for her most generous gift. Touched by the expressions of gratitude, she wrote to David, saying that he would be a reflection of her beloved husband.

As David read the letter, he was moved by the spiritual parallels in the situation. Just as Jesus gave His life so that we might have eternal life, Serafino's death had given him a chance to live. Just as Sonni looked to him to reflect the life of her husband, our new spiritual birth allows us to reflect the life of Jesus within us.

David felt such a debt of gratitude to Sonni for giving him the gift of life, he spoke with his cousin, Ann Kiemel Anderson, the author of several books, about telling the story of the gift. Initially, Ann did not think that the story of a liver transplant would be very meaningful to a wide audience. However, sensing the leading of the Lord, she went ahead. Her book, *This is a Story*

About God, is all about impossible things becoming possible with the help of Jesus. —DRL

May J be diligent to follow You. Take care of the brokenhearted and heal the sick.

✺ 70 ✺

Ruth Ann Reddon

New-Found Freedom in Christ!

Memories... if only the bad ones could disappear forever. Yet there they remain, deeply embedded in the subconscious, ready to reappear unbeckoned when least expected. Hauntingly, they conjure up unwanted emotions; confining prisoners to chains of the past.

For many years, Ruth Ann Reddon was one of these prisoners. As a young child, she vividly remembers the devastation of being told she was unwanted. As one who can identify with others who have experienced the pain of being unloved and rejected, she confides, "At the age of three, my world collapsed." The following crucial developmental years continued to be equally destructive.

Ruth Ann did all she could to prevent the destructive forces from destroying her life and marriage as an adult. Yet the familiar feelings of rejection, loneliness, and depression only remained. Even the medication prescribed by her doctor for depression could not erase the years of pain and neglect.

With hindsight, Ruth Ann now understands that all her efforts to change things only brought temporary relief. "I worked so hard at trying to fix my life and marriage, but couldn't do it without God's help," she acknowledges. It was at this point that the Lord began to change things – and it all started with the ministry of *100 Huntley Street.*

"One night when I was very depressed, I spoke with a Crossroads prayer partner named Katherine. She took the time to talk to me and pray for me. She even prayed for the restoration of my marriage. I didn't tell her that my marriage was in trouble – the Holy Spirit led her."

During the conversation, Ruth Ann was encouraged to attend a recommended church in her area. So the following morning, she contacted the church. Within a few days, she was taken to a women's meeting by someone from her neighbourhood. Ruth Ann adds, "And through her, many other doors have opened that I never would have believed possible!"

In the meantime, Ruth Ann's husband Lyle became aware of the dramatic changes taking place as the Holy Spirit began to transform her. When invited to attend a Bible study, to her astonishment, he replied yes. Ruth Ann rejoiced for she knew that God was answering her prayers: "I had been praying for over a year for Lyle. On October 1, 1995, he accepted Christ in his heart. What a glorious day!"

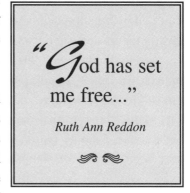

"*God* has set me free..."

Ruth Ann Reddon

The Lord has performed many other wonders in her life as well. Ruth Ann joyfully counts her blessings as she says, "God has set me free from those painful memories of the past. I laid all my problems at Jesus' feet, and in return, He has given me peace and joy. I give Him all the glory. He is an awesome God!" —KS

☙ *71* ❧

Fabian & Wilma Connolly

A New Kind of Freedom

Having served over 13 years in prison for a variety of offenses, including bank-robbing and safe-cracking, Fabian Connolly was out of jail. In or out, however, his heart was empty. He didn't care whether he lived or died. With no compassion for anyone, he thought nothing of breaking the jaw of any homeless street person who might wander in his way.

In 1985, Fabian heard that his old partner in crime and prison time, Alex McEachern was back in Toronto. When Alex managed to get hold of Fabian, he invited him to a Full Gospel Business Men's Fellowship International (FGBMFI) meeting where he was booked to speak. He had "found Jesus." Skeptical, Fabian accepted his invitation. This had to be good.

Once at the FGBMFI banquet, Fabian's discomfort was dimmed by his appreciation of the food. They didn't get grub like this on the inside. Then it was time for the speaker. As Alex took his place behind the podium, Fabian saw the most glorious bright light. It was Jesus, standing behind Alex in the midst of a golden glow – the most beautiful, purest, most precious sight Fabian had ever seen. Thinking that maybe he was seeing things, he wiped his eyes a few times, but the vision remained. When Alex's message was finally over, Fabian was the first one down to the front to give his life to Jesus Christ.

At that moment, Fabian's life began to change. The Lord told him to go out into the streets to feed the hungry and homeless. Fabian went, but didn't want to be there. He hated people like that. He didn't want to feed them. He wanted to beat them up.

However, as he was obedient, God gradually showed him that it was because he had been one of them that he felt hatred for them. It wasn't really that he hated them – he hated what he had been. From that point, he began to feed and love the homeless into the kingdom.

That same year, Fabian met a girl named Wilma. Partying and getting drunk every weekend, all she cared about was having a good time. The more she tried to have fun, however, the less fun she had. Finally disgusted with herself, she said, "That's it. I am not going to drink anymore." That night, she went to bed, said her prayers (as was her custom) and went to sleep. During the night, she was awakened and saw Jesus standing, looking at her from the foot of her bed. Jumping up, she began to pray and has never had another drink from that day to this.

Six months later, Wilma went to hear Alex speak and gave her life to Jesus. Transformed, she was filled by the sweetest peace she has ever known. Suddenly, she loved everybody. No matter how hard an exterior might be, she could see through it to a hurting heart that just needed Jesus.

Fabian and Wilma were married and began to spend their time on the streets, showing the love of Jesus to the homeless. Gradually, they began a systematic feeding program called, The Brotherhood of Christians, which at one point necessitated pawning Wilma's wedding rings to buy the food (she eventually got them back). According to Wilma, "What good are wedding rings when you know somebody is starving? It's better to get some food for them than to wear diamonds."

With the assistance of other caring individuals, Fabian and Wilma now have a good number of buses across Canada, with volunteers taking soup, meals, clothing and the Good News of Jesus to street people. Not forgetting those behind bars, they also have a faithful prison ministry. The riches they will one day reap far outweigh any gold that any bank could ever yield. —DRL

✌ *72* ✌

Melanie Serr

Sweet Sixteen

Standing at the threshold of adulthood, for most teens, life is filled with excitement and expectations. But how does a young person cope with life when terrifying news strikes? On November 24, 1996, one day before her 16th birthday, Melanie Serr was told the unthinkable. She had a tumour on her brain.

Instead of allowing the life-threatening circumstances to overtake her, she anchored in God. "I knew He was taking care of me and that I was in His hands. God gave me His peace. I felt as if He was saying, 'It's going to be okay.'"

In August of 1998, Melanie had undergone brain surgery, but unfortunately the doctors were only able to remove 70 percent of the tumour without causing irreversible brain damage. The statistics were very grim – the five-year survival rate is only 20 percent.

Melanie and her family were faced with a choice: chemotherapy and radiation, or a relatively new treatment known as "antineoplastons" offered by a clinic in Houston, Texas. Because this treatment was approved by neither the FDA in the United States nor by Canada's Health Board, the cost, at $15,000 Canadian a month, was prohibitive. In order to go this unconventional route, a trust fund for Melanie had to be established to help her family cover the costs. The revenue from her own music CD, *Surround Me*, contributed toward the expenses and opened the doors for her to minister to others.

Almost one year later, in June 1999, with a catheter in her heart cavity, Melanie visited *100 Huntley Street* for the first time with some unusual equipment. "These tubes are hooked up to the valves of my heart and the treatment just flows through," she explains. "Attached to the tubes are two bags containing medication: one breaks down the cancer cell wall and the other builds it up. In other words, the treatment reprograms the cancer cells back into normal healthy cells so the disease can die off naturally. It doesn't destroy any healthy cells in the body."

Many viewers across Canada prayed for Melanie, and God answered! Just four months later, on October 8, 1999, Melanie revisited the *100 Huntley Street* program. This time she brought copies of her medical records. According to the documents from McMaster University Medical Centre, dated June 15, 1999, "There is no evidence on the PET scan of recurrent tumour." She also presented an

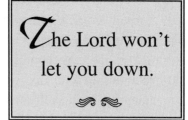

The Lord won't let you down.

MRI report from Foothills Hospital in Calgary confirming the diagnosis.

"When we spoke to the radiologist, he said, 'There is no sign of cancer here.' I was so thrilled," says Melanie. "I was just waiting for this moment! In my heart I knew I was healed. Now it was confirmed in the world."

During her October '99 visit, Melanie was still on follow-up oral medication. But she came to encourage others who may be dealing with life's difficult circumstances: "Don't focus on the problem; don't claim that mountain as yours. Claim Jesus as the Lord of your life. He's not going to turn you away. He will give you His peace. Jesus came so we could have health. And for those who are at wit's end – persevere! The Lord is faithful and will never let you down." —HS

✆ 73 ✆

Rhonda London

Live!

At the age of 11, Rhonda London's life changed. Until then, life growing up in the Ottawa Valley was relatively unremarkable. She was involved in all of the regular kid stuff, had a dog and a pony, a loving family and believed that there was a God. What more was there to life?

The change began when Rhonda's mother began to watch *100 Huntley Street*. Coming to know Jesus through the program, she introduced her daughter to Him. As the little girl listened to her mother, the realization that she could actually have a two-way relationship with God was almost shocking to her. It was a life-changing, light bulb moment. Never had she even thought about the possibility that He had a personal interest in her individually, or that He had a special plan for her life.

Asking Jesus into her heart that day, Rhonda has never looked back. A few years later, with an interest in journalism and broadcasting, she discovered that Evangel College, a Christian liberal arts college in Springfield, Missouri, had an excellent reputation for its journalism program.

In 1989, diploma tucked neatly under her arm, she headed back to the Ottawa Valley, to CHRO. Initially hired as a weekend radio news anchor, she was gradually promoted to full-time TV reporter and TV news anchor. For nine years, she honed her broadcasting skills, eventually producing and anchoring a one-hour news show.

In 1995, having felt that her Christian walk was unfruitful, she had an "amazing breakthrough," experiencing the fullness of the Holy Spirit. God impressed her with the depth of His love and His great desire to bless His children.

Secure in her position and loving her work, she was somewhat surprised at the restlessness that began to grow within her. She knew that God was telling her that it was time to move on, but she had no idea where she would go.

With no knowledge of her own program, *Rhonda London Live!* awaiting her at CTS in Burlington, she began to pack.

Months later came the offer of her own show on the new Christian CTS station. Rhonda dusted off the boxes waiting in her hallway and moved to Burlington. *Rhonda London Live!* is a daily program driven by current events, "real issues that affect real people." With daily guests and phone lines open to callers, it is interactive television at its finest – a dynamic interplay of informative guests and probing telephone questions, all resting on the well of God's wisdom from which Rhonda can draw at the nudging of the Holy Spirit.

> *A*s the little girl listened to her mother, the realization that she could actually have a two-way relationship with God was almost shocking to her.

Unmarried when she arrived at CTS, Rhonda had a heart for "singles" ministry. However, God had more than a job waiting for her. Love was there in the person of a handsome producer, Ray-David Glenn. As of October 27, 2001, Rhonda's interest switched to "newlyweds." —DRL

✌ *74* ✌

Jody Cross

A *Lifeline for Souls*

"God, please don't let my dad die!" cried the traumatized young 13-year-old. The sight of his father's motionless body hooked up to intravenous and monitoring apparatus was much more than he could bear. For several weeks, the life of his father – once a strong and seemingly invincible man – hung in delicate balance.

This incident, even though it occurred more than 23 years ago, left a strong impression on Jody Cross. Today, a father himself, he recounts how the events surrounding the accident ultimately altered the course of his own life.

I grew up in a non-Christian home," he confides. "There was a lot of love in our family until alcoholism became a significant factor." After many unhappy years and unresolved conflicts, Jody's parents eventually divorced. The resulting confusion he experienced merely added to his overall sense of emptiness, or what he now describes as a "spiritual vacuum."

In reflection, he says, "Unfortunately, I got involved in a lot of things that teenagers do. And although I didn't consider myself a bad individual, now looking back, I realize those things were not pleasing to God nor very healthy for me either."

In 1978, when his father suffered from a very serious head injury, Jody was faced with the possibility of permanently losing his dad whom he looked up to for affirmation and strength. "It was a real crisis; a turning point in my life," he adds. "I didn't want my dad to die. God was really my only hope – my last hope."

To Jody's amazement, God did a miracle. After an agonizing six-week wait, his father regained consciousness. Step by step, in gradual stages, Jody began to witness progress: "First he was able to hear, then he was able to see – and within nine months, he was released from the hospital."

Despite these remarkable events, it wasn't until March of 1980 that Jody's life truly began to change.

"This one particular morning while watching *100 Huntley Street*, I listened as a gentleman gave his testimony," he explains. "I had never heard the Gospel before – the simple message that Jesus Christ loved me and died for me. I was convinced at this point. I knew I needed Him to change my life and was ready to give Him a chance."

Jody then made a decision that saved his life. In fact, he describes it with an interesting analogy: "I was like a drowning man. I needed someone to rescue me and pull me back into the lifeboat."

Since the day Jesus rescued him from drowning in the turbulent waters of life, Jody is determined to give his all to God through his role in ministry as a youth pastor: "I want to be involved – investing my life in eternal things and impacting people's lives spiritually." —KS

> "*I* had never heard the Gospel before – the simple message that Jesus Christ loved me and died for me. I knew I needed Him to change my life."
>
> *Jody Cross*

～ 75 ～

Terry MacDonald-Cadieux

Fast Track to Heaven

At a time when most little girls are daintily taking their first toddling steps, Terry MacDonald drove her first go-cart. When the red-headed two-year-old got that first hit of speed, she became an adrenaline junkie. Good thing she got saved at the ripe old age of four!

With her dad and brothers both race car drivers, Terry's first speed thrill was not her last. Hanging around the cars, she was a quick study and her knowledge of engines soon won her enough respect to be accepted as one of the boys in the pits. No languishing lily, she loved nothing better than the stink of exhausts, the pulsing throb of heavy engines and the roar from the stands when a car was headed down the back stretch.

In her twelveth summer, Terry rededicated her life to Jesus and she and her brother were baptized by immersion. Having thus determined her values in life, her teen years were filled with wholesome activities, not the least of which was the development of her love for sports.

Prayer changes things.

～ ～

These were a huge part of Terry's university life in Florida. The only female on the men's flag football team, she tried out for the Miami Dolphins and then declined the position. Having allowed sports the preeminent place in her life, a car accident when on the way to a party with a group of friends woke her up to the fact that she had gotten off track. The very next day, she recommitted her life to God and became active in her church's youth group.

Following university graduation, Terry returned home to Canada. Ready to pursue her love of professional auto racing, she found another love – her crew chief! Once married, the two charged towards the checkered flag in every area of their lives.

In her first six years competing in Canada, Terry made history as the highest ranking female in ASN Canada FIA Professional Road Racing and has earned many awards. Her unique personality, strong beliefs and comfort in front of a camera have propelled her into product sponsoring, speaking, journalism and production of her own video, *Terry's Crash Course,* a car maintenance guide for women. With her marketing skills, she works hard on promoting herself and giving her sponsors the very best exposure possible.

In 1997, Terry suffered a major accident at Road Atlanta. Racing at over 150 m.p.h., her car was tapped from behind, rolled and smashed into the wall, breaking her C-2 vertebrae in three places. Immediately, her father called several churches and a prayer chain was formed. People began praying all across the country. Although told that she would be in a halo and body cast for 13 weeks, to be followed by a neck brace, Terry was back driving the PPG pace car only 12 weeks after the accident! With only four percent chance of surviving such an injury and then only three percent of not being permanently confined to a wheelchair, she knows that God intervened and restored her for His purposes.

Now the official pace car driver for the INDY car series, Terry says that she wouldn't even consider driving if she were not a Christian. Because she knows that earth isn't really her home anyway, she has no fear. Beginning each day with a song God gives her, she spends a half hour in devotions with Him before her day is off to the races. —DRL

✍ 76 ✍

Dianne Williamson

The Missing Piece

With eyes full of wonder, the youngsters listen as children's church leader Dianne Williamson teaches the Bible story lesson. Impressed upon their receptive hearts is the fact that God loves them very much and has promised to be with them all the days of their lives – just as He was with Daniel, whose life was spared from the den of hungry ravenous lions.

The truth of God's power and love was initially introduced to Dianne when she was just a young child herself. At the tender age of four, her mother instilled the knowledge of God as the Creator of the universe and of all creation, which she enjoyed learning about while growing up.

"At that young age, I sensed God's hand on my life," she says. "And through different landmarks, God demonstrated to me that He was real." Like the time she had contracted polio. Overcome with fear, the ten-year-old announced aloud, "This could be the end of my life." Reassuringly, Dianne's mother explained to her that God is the Great Physician and had the power to heal. So, as a child, she simply prayed and asked Him to heal her.

"I had this simple childlike faith that God could do it, and to my amazement, He did! In a matter of about one minute, I felt the healing presence of the Lord. The warmth that filled my body started at the top of my head and went right down to the tips of my toes.... I was totally healed!"

Even though Dianne had experienced the powerful healing touch of God, as a teenager she was eager to discover what the world had to offer. At age 18, she ventured to the big city of Toronto. Shortly after, she was reunited with a former beau –

the young university graduate from her hometown whom she married the following year. Sentimentally she adds, "I knew without a doubt that he was the man for me."

As a happily married wife, and eventually mother of a beautiful baby boy, things couldn't be better... so she thought. Then one morning, while turning on the television set in search of a suitable children's program for her young son, she accidentally came across *100 Huntley Street*. From that moment onward, Dianne was soon to begin a brand new chapter of her life.

With joy she explains how a "personal" Jesus was introduced to her for the very first time: "When I turned that channel on and heard

> ## "*I* had this simple child-like faith that God could do it, and to my amazement, He did!"
>
> *Dianne Williamson*

what David Mainse was saying about having a personal relationship with Jesus, in my spirit I became excited. That really was the piece missing in my life. Although I knew He existed, I had never invited Him in – I didn't know I could. It was like turning a light on for me!"

Dianne's curiosity about *100 Huntley Street* and her eagerness to learn more about the Person of Jesus compelled her to watch the program again the following day. She adds, "That was the day I got down on my knees and asked the Lord to come into my life. And I have never looked back one moment since that day!" —KS

❧ 77 ❧

Bill Wilson

A Lighthouse in the Ghetto

"I can't do this anymore. You wait here." Fourteen-year-old Bill Wilson's alcoholic mother had reached a dead end. Her life hadn't worked and she was no longer willing to pretend at any ability to parent. She was about to simply drop out of Bill's life.

As she walked away, Bill watched her go. When she was finally out of sight, his eyes stared glassily ahead. He thought some jumbled thoughts and simply kept breathing. With his father dead and his mother now gone, it was all he had left in life to do. Finally, he sat down on the curb. She had said to wait.

Three days later, Bill was still sitting on the curb. Dave Rudenis, an auto mechanic from the church, came along, picked him up and took him under his wing. Bill's mother never returned.

That summer, Dave offered to pay for Bill's tuition at a summer youth camp. While there, Bill heard for the first time that Jesus had died for him. The message went deep, touched the pain in the young boy's heart and poured oil into the gaping wound. With heart and soul, Bill responded, giving his life to Christ at the camp.

In 1968, Bill was 19 years old. While many others of his generation wove flowers in their hair and sang ballads about peace, Bill understood its meaning in a way many of them never would.

With a burning desire to share God's peace with broken-hearted young people, his vision for spiritual lighthouses in local communities grew. Bill believed that if he could be instrumental in changing one generation for Christ in places where people were trapped by their circumstances, those circumstances would have no hold on the new generation. In Bill's words: "No child would ever come out bad if they had at least one person who really cared."

Once ordained, Bill served until the age of 30 as a children's and youth pastor. Wherever he went, that church became the fastest growing congregation in the state. With a sense of urgency to reclaim humanity for Christ, he ministered in every state in America with a challenge to the church of today.

Now, as the pastor of The Metro Assembly of God in Brooklyn, New York, Bill has continued to fix his sights on reaching the masses. Focussing particularly on the human wasteland of America's forgotten inner cities, his mission is to find and rescue the children who are trapped in the despair of broken relationships, poverty, the drug culture and every other ill of society. "There is a battle for the lives of these children," he explains. "Winning their precious lives takes extraordinary time and materials. It's not easy, especially surrounded by the violence and poverty of New York City ghettos."

As founder and director of Metro Inner City Children's Campaign, he reaches over 20,000 people each week. Using the latest in internet and multimedia technology, his sermons are available with the click of a mouse in homes around the world.

Bill's fire and commitment to evangelism and discipleship of all ages is contagious. Seeing his inner city bus ministry overflowing with children who can't wait to get to his enormous Yogi Bear Sunday School – then go home and encourage their defeated parents with stories of the love of Jesus – is the best lesson in effective evangelism.

It is the prayer of Bill and his dedicated team of co-workers that the vision, which has compelled them to reach the masses, may become alive in the heart of every Christian. Just as the decision to take the love of Christ to the ghettos of New York has transformed countless lives, that same love of Christ needs to be taken to every city around the world. —DRL

> ## "*There is a battle for the lives of these children.*"   *Bill Wilson*

You must be motivated to care.

≈ 78 ≈

Al & Madeline Harvey

"Christ is the Answer!"

The bold white letters on the front of the building caught the attention of Al and Madeline Harvey as they travelled along Interstate 75 in their leased transport truck. The words read, "Christ is the Answer."

Al laughed as he steered the truck along the freeway. "You give me the question and I'll tell you if Christ is the answer!" he said jokingly to Madeline. At the time, they didn't realize that the very words on that sign were soon to have significant meaning in their lives.

Prior to discovering this truth, they travelled along some rocky roads. Madeline states, "Back in '88, everything was upside-down. I had broken my ankle which put me in a wheelchair for eight weeks. We were also having money problems. I became very bitter and built a high wall around myself.... I felt there had to be something more to life than what we had."

In her quest for "something more," Madeline found herself intrigued with *100 Huntley Street*. She says, "A young woman by the name of Diane Alimena-Schaetzle stood in front of the prayer lines offering a different way of life; a way that was available to me. All I had to do was pray with her and invite Jesus Christ into my heart." That day – February 7, 1989 – Madeline made the life-changing decision to accept Jesus as her Lord.

The transformation that took place during the following months was living proof to her family that God was real and at work in her life. Over a period of time, Madeline's bad language cleaned up. To her surprise, she even gave up smoking which she acknowledges was a miracle in itself. "I thank God for taking that bondage out of my life," she adds.

Although Madeline didn't say very much to Al about her new relationship with the Lord, her actions spoke louder than words. Sure enough, all the years of disbelief crumbled when his spiritual eyes were opened.

While travelling by himself in the "rig" along the usual route of Interstate 75 on December 4, 1989, something wonderfully strange took place as Al read the words of the sign he had mocked many times before: "Christ is the Answer."

"Being as low as I was spiritually, I cried out to the Lord," he says. "I made up my mind that if Christ was the answer and if God was real, that's what I needed. It was there God spoke to my heart and made me realize that I needed Him in my life. So I accepted the Lord at that point, not realizing my wife had an army behind her praying for me at *100 Huntley Street* and the little church recommended to us."

With joy Madeline acknowledges, "Crossroads referred us to the church where we are both serving today. Al plays the guitar in the band during the service. It's also a joy to share the Word of God and pray together.... I thank Him for the many things He has done in our lives!" —KS

ॐ 79 ॐ

Michael Peterson

A Song of Strength and Hope

Everybody's got "stuff." Take Michael Peterson for example. He has a whole list:

- almost aborted by his mother at four months gestation
- sexually abused as a child
- parents divorced
- father murdered by a disgruntled business partner
- dyslexic and labelled a "slow-learner"
- very low self-esteem
- trusted no one
- step-father committed suicide when Michael was 15

Why? Why did this talented, innocent boy have to endure heartbreaking misery when his childhood should have been filled with happiness and comfort? Why do we all have painful challenges of one sort or another?

No one knows the details but God. This world is full of pain and suffering. According to the Genesis account, it has been that way ever since sin entered the world. When that happened, everything was affected. Weeds grew, parents started fighting, the price of clothing went up and kids killed each other.

Sin does not happen in a vacuum. The longer it has been in the world, the more complicated life gets with its effects. Every little baby on earth is born into circumstances created by the actions or inactions, choices, behaviours and attitudes of those around him or her. As the child grows, his or her choices and

DNA are thrown into the mix – all adding up to that person's package of "stuff." Even as one traces the genealogy of Christian families, suffering is found, because here on earth, it rains on the just and on the unjust.

It's not just the individual list that really matters. It's what we do with it. That's where choice comes in. We either run around in circles trying to "keep our stuff together," or we give it to God and watch Him bring good out of what Satan has meant to use to destroy us – waking up to the fact that each challenge that God has allowed on our list is a nudge from Him to look up, believe that His Son came to save us from evil and enter into eternal life in the place He prepared for us. Never, never, ever, did God will that humans should go to hell, the place He prepared for Satan. It is not His will that any should perish (2 Peter 3:9). However, by not consciously choosing God, the lost choose to go with Satan by default.

Having become so accustomed to pain in his life that he didn't feel comfortable without it, Michael constantly set himself up for failure. With no familiar frame of reference for success, he was addicted to crisis. As a victim of abuse, he had tried to get control of the situation by blaming himself. Despite his good self-image, his self-esteem was almost non-existent. It wasn't until God showed him that the abuse wasn't his fault, that the healing could really begin. Until then, he didn't know that the past doesn't have to control the future.

God uses people. In Michael's life, one of those was his football coach. By helping Michael to establish tangible goals in his life, a sense of purpose and satisfaction began to emerge. His introduction to Jesus brought things into even clearer focus.

When Michael finally handed the broken pieces of his life to Him, God took them gently in His hands and, one by one, showed Michael that, although He had allowed each fragment to be broken, He would restore and meaningfully place every piece into the magnificent pattern He had designed for Michael's life. But healing takes time. Because of the distrust that had built up through the years, it was difficult for Michael to eventually commit to marriage. For the same reasons, it was hard for him to thoroughly give his life to God. However, just as years of his wife's faithfulness proved her love for him, God proved Himself over and over to Michael.

In 1983, he travelled across the country with the *Power Team*, performing feats of strength to attract crowds with the purpose of evangelism in schools and wherever doors opened.

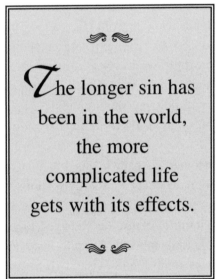

The longer sin has been in the world, the more complicated life gets with its effects.

Having begun to sing at the age of five, Michael's music ministry began to grow and now is recognized by its inspiring lyrics and melodies. His debut album contained two "Top 30" singles and earned both Grammy and Dove nominations. His music and testimony are skillfully woven together to focus on the profound connection between personal and spiritual relationships with a powerful message of hope. Although his past hasn't changed, Michael now sees God's hand through it all and uses it to encourage others. He sings, *"I believe He accepts who I am today, but He loves me too much to leave me that way."* —DRL

You can still have scars and not bleed anymore. Allow emotions to surface. The church must be there to walk you through the hurts.

✎ *80* ✎

Diane Finley-McCooeye

Reason To Celebrate Life!

The glow of the candle, lit in the bathroom, could not dispel the darkness of her agonizing soul – longing for an end to grief and depression. Distraught, Diane Finley-McCooeye felt so much inner turmoil that she uttered a scream for help, calling on the all-powerful Name of Jesus.

Shortly after her mother's death in 1994, Diane no longer wanted to live. In order to escape her relentless misery, she carefully planned a way of escape: suicide. "I just want to be with mom," she reasoned to herself.

Diane vividly remembers when she was told the shattering news that her mother was in the last stages of angina. Her initial reaction to the doctor's prognosis was that of shock: "I remember leaving the doctor's office that day and thinking, How could you have her in the final stages when I need her forever?"

Unable to bear the suffering of her mother's painful illness, Diane found herself becoming a very angry person. Soon her anger toward God and others was uncontrollable. "I became the type of person who yelled at people," she admits.

Emotionally fragile, Diane began to do things that were out of character for her, and she lost her job as a result. The losses she experienced within a short period of time became overwhelming. With concern, her boyfriend Ken suggested she see her doctor who prescribed medication for depression. However, her mind was made up. It was time to finalize her plans.

"The day that I went to see our family doctor, I wrote letters to all my loved ones," she says. "I was going to end my life. I even prearranged my funeral." Just before carrying through with her carefully contemplated suicide, however, Diane screamed out, "Jesus, if You're real, where are You when I need You?"

At that precise moment the doorbell rang. Assuming it was a neighbour checking up on her, Diane answered the door. To her surprise, there stood an old friend. Brian said to her, "I had to deliver a letter down the road and turned in here because I heard that you were in trouble and probably needed some help."

After talking with her for a few minutes, Brian went on his way. Suddenly, Diane felt compelled to sit in her mother's favourite chair and watch television for a moment – something she rarely did. She switched on the TV set and there was *100 Huntley Street.* She listened closely to what David Mainse was saying over the airwaves: "If you are thinking of ending your life, don't do it. Give your life to Jesus."

Diane started to cry, "But I know Jesus...." David continued to explain how a person may know Him with mere head knowledge, but not in the heart. As he spoke, the Holy Spirit revealed the need for Diane to give her heart to Jesus by inviting Him to be Lord of her life.

On April 4, 1995, she called the Crossroads Ministry Centre to give her life to Christ. "And He has made me amazingly new!" she adds. "When I turned myself completely over to Him in total surrender – holding nothing back – He washed me clean. Not only does He forgive everything, He doesn't even remember."

Since Diane has relinquished her life to the Lord, she has been given a whole new reason to celebrate life! On October 5, 1995, she married Ken and together they began a business. Their work now provides the means for them to help save the lives of precious people through their Crossroads partnership. She also spends many hours as a palliative care volunteer in her local hospital, bringing the joy and love of Jesus to chronic care patients. Diane is right when she says, "Life is so good once you totally surrender to Jesus!" —KS

✺ *81* ✺

Kate Convissor

Young Widow

"When death encircled me – when I studied my husband's face in his coffin while our fifth child waited to be born – then I learned of God," writes Kate Convissor in her book, *Young Widow.* "At the time of my widowhood, when my need was desperate, I learned that grace was enough."

As a teenager, Kate had struggled with her faith. She no longer felt that it answered the "big questions" in life for her. It wasn't until she went on a high school retreat where she was introduced to a loving, intimate God, that she found the answers she needed.

For several years, Kate lived in Detroit's inner city where, through her prayer group, she was involved with the city's poor and desperate. Through those years, she learned not only about the fragile beauty and pain of the world's outcasts, but about the faithfulness of God.

When her husband, the father of her five children, drowned in a tragic fishing accident, Kate embarked on a journey from agonizing grief to wholeness. For months, she could not understand that her husband was not coming back.

Her children, ranging in age from four to eleven (she was four months pregnant at the time of the drowning), did not initially express their feelings. They were quiet, not even crying more than usual. In time, however, their feelings began to surface. Under the solemn exterior of the four-year-old, guilt emerged from believing that he should have told his dad not to go fishing. Gradually, through the process of healing, Kate's children experienced the Fatherhood of God in a very special way.

As God led Kate and her family through the grieving process, giving them the strength they needed, she knew they were learning lessons that could bring hope to others in similar circumstances. *Young Widow* deals with such issues as: raising children alone, how children understand death and incorporate grief into their lives, reforging an identity, maintaining life's responsibilities, re-entering the world as a single person, remarriage and creating a new life. The outstanding message of the book is that God is enough for any crisis.

Kate is now remarried and lives in Grand Rapids, Michigan, with her husband, Craig Convissor, and six children. —DRL

❧ *82* ❧

Sheri-Lynn Keller

A Generation of Destiny

The sweltering heat of the midday sun scorches the metal exterior of the bus as it journeys to another one of the many impoverished villages in Mexico. Shortly after arriving at its destination, a woman and child run excitedly toward the vehicle. "Could someone pray for us?" she asks in Spanish. Soon other villagers arrive – young and old alike – to receive food, clothing and ministry tracts.

Nothing, not even the heat of the day, could squelch the enthusiasm of young Sheri-Lynn Keller who busily hands out toys and ministers God's love to the children. To her, the joy of reaching others for Christ is worth it all.

"God's love goes beyond language barriers," Sheri explains. Referring to our modern-day culture, she is convinced that His love and salvation even breaks the language barriers between generations. This truth is real to her as she came to salvation in Christ while only a child herself:

"When I was five years old, I stayed at my grandmother's house for Christmas. Before anyone else woke up, I went downstairs and turned on the TV to watch some cartoons. *100 Huntley Street* was on. David Mainse presented the Gospel in a way that was easily understood. Suddenly God's presence and peace filled the room. I remember responding, 'Jesus, I give You my heart.' It was that simple."

Ever since the day of her salvation, God's hand has remained on Sheri's life. "Even when I went through hard times in high school, Jesus was there all the time," she acknowledges. "He guided me through and gave me the strength I needed."

Sheri knows from first-hand experience some of the difficulties that teens face. For about a year, she struggled with feelings of inferiority and low self-esteem – to the point of being suicidal. "When I was really upset, I called the Crossroads prayer line. The prayer partner prayed for me and helped me to calm down," she adds. "I realized that God loved me the way I was and had a special purpose for my life."

At 22 years of age, Sheri now conveys God's unconditional love to hurting teens in her community. "When the Lord opened my eyes spiritually to the needs of youth, I began interceding for them," she says. "The world tells them the 'Generation X' message: There are no jobs... there is no future... and there is no hope. My heart is broken for them."

In order to reach out to aimless and disillusioned teens, Sheri uses her gift of music to communicate God's truth. "Music is definitely like a language to them. Through music they can know that there is more to live for, there *is hope*, there *is God!"*

Since the day Sheri discovered the Lord, the reality of God's presence in her life has shaped her destiny: "Jesus is the centre of my life. I live and breath for Him. I want His love to flow through me. Sometimes I wonder where I would have been without Him. I am a life that has been changed!" —KS

✍ *83* ✍

Nizar Shaheen

"Thou art Mine."

When Ellen, daughter of David and Norma-Jean Mainse, was taking her first toddler steps, a dark-haired little boy played near the shores of the Sea of Galilee.

Raised in Cana, where his family has lived for many generations, Nizar attended the Roman Catholic school. God, like the flag billowing in the breeze, was part of the fabric of his life. He had a vague sense of wanting to serve Him, but like a flash of electricity, the thought would come and then be gone. Five minutes later, he would have forgotten his desire.

During his teen years, Nizar's natural athletic ability came to the fore and he began to box. Every day he would run from Cana to the Sea of Galilee, a distance of 15 miles. Plunging into the slate blue waters, he would swim vigorously and then run back.

With laser vision on his goals, it was no surprise to anyone that he became a champion boxer. Greatly admired in his community, Nizar's heart became very proud – but beneath the proud exterior burned a heart of hatred born of centuries of prejudice.

As a university student at Haifa, a friend asked him to go to hear an American missionary speak. The missionary asked Nizar whether he had accepted Jesus as Saviour. With no answer, the question hung limply in Nizar's mind.

But God continued to pursue him, miraculously protecting him in three major accidents. One time, he fell from a mosque roof onto his head, landing in a small clearing. Breaking his hands, he heard a voice say, "Nizar, do not fear for *I have called thee by thy name; thou art Mine.*" Following two car accidents, he again heard a voice saying, *"I have called thee by thy name; thou art Mine."* On the third occasion, God spoke powerfully to him about his surrender to Jesus Christ as Saviour and Lord. Audibly, Nizar heard, *"I have called thee by thy name; thou art Mine."* In 1979, at the age of 20, he was led to go to a church where revival meetings were being held and he accepted the Lord. From that time, there has been no turning back.

With an enormous hunger for the Word, he began to devour the Scriptures. In Isaiah 43:1, he was startled to find the words that he had heard God speak directly to him every time his life had been spared: *"I have called thee by thy name; thou art Mine."* Applying the same tremendous drive he had exerted in his athletic training, he read and reread the Bible many times each year.

In 1981, during a three-month Youth With A Mission course, Nizar had a powerful experience with the Holy Spirit which caused him, for the first time in his life, to really love the Jewish people as he did his own Arab brothers and sisters.

As a student at the American University in Israel, Ellen was studying archaeology and Hebrew. It wasn't long before she and Nizar knew that their friendship held a wonderful promise for the future. One day, David got a call from Nizar asking for Ellen's hand in marriage. Apologizing for not having a go-between, as is customary in that part of the world, Nizar was unaware that the work of a go-between had already been accomplished by the Holy Spirit. When they had first met Nizar, Norma-Jean and

David had each known, independently of the other, that Nizar was the man Ellen would marry.

On May 21, 1983, in a magnificent wedding in Cana of Galilee, Ellen and Nizar were wed. It was a never-to-be-forgotten ceremony with Nizar arriving on a magnificent white stallion, televised for all the world to see.

Following the wedding, the two went to Belgium to study at Continental Bible College. Finally equipped with a degree in theology from Brussels, Nizar had a vision for full-time ministry. Although he knew nothing about broadcasting when he first met Ellen, he spoke in faith that he would produce an Arabic television program.

Starting with a single pilot, *Light for all Nations* now reaches the immigrant population from Arab countries here in the west and also covers many countries through Middle East Television. Known by many who hear him as a "teacher's teacher," Nizar is the president and host of *Light for all Nations* as well as host of the very popular *Let There Be Light* video series produced by *100 Huntley Street*. He and Ellen now reside in Canada with their six children. —DRL

When you are fellowshipping with the Lord daily and reading His Word daily, He will give you His will for your life.

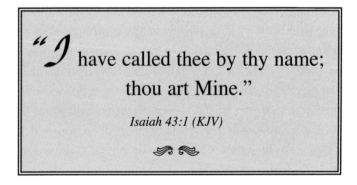

"*I* have called thee by thy name;
thou art Mine."

Isaiah 43:1 (KJV)

～ *84* ～

Michelle Gillette

Restoring Broken Dreams

Michelle Gillette curled up on the chesterfield in tears that spring morning of '96. Hearing her children's cries for their father from the other room only intensified her own pain. Overcome with depression and anxiety, Michelle knew she had reached the lowest point of her life.

"It was a very difficult time," Michelle recalls. "My husband Bruce and I were separated and heading for divorce. I had moved into an apartment with our three young children. I honestly believe if *100 Huntley Street* wasn't there that day, I would have committed suicide."

Prior to marrying Bruce, Michelle experienced a lot of emotional abuse while in a former relationship. The hurtful words spoken years earlier by an ex-boyfriend kept taunting her. "As a result," she admits, "I was always on my guard. I never wanted to be hurt again."

From the beginning of their marriage, bitterness and resentment began to surface. This, along with financial stress, attributed to a rocky start. "We soon began tearing each other down instead of supporting one another," she says. "And we argued about every little thing – silly things that aren't worth arguing about."

This destructive behaviour slowly eroded their marriage, and divorce seemed to be the only solution – that is, until Michelle tuned into Life-Changing Television: "I can remember changing the channels on the TV not knowing what I was even looking for and, at the same time, thinking about killing myself so I could stop the pain. *100 Huntley Street* was on. I can't recall what the program was about. All I can remember is the peace on the faces of those on the program and their lovely voices....

"I wrote down the phone number that was on the screen. When I called the first time, the line was busy. But something in my heart kept saying, 'Keep trying, Michelle. Keep trying.' Finally I got through to a wonderful person on the other end. Yet, because of my tears, I couldn't speak. The prayer partner sensed my need and began to pray for me."

Besides praying for reconciliation, the Crossroads prayer partner helped Michelle to realize something of even greater importance: her need of a personal relationship with Jesus. "When I asked the Lord to come into my heart and my life," she states, "He lifted off the bitterness and anger. I felt a sense of peace and hope in a situation that seemed so hopeless. For the first time, I felt worthy of happiness and love."

To ensure Michelle received further ministry, the Crossroads Ministry Centre contacted a follow-up pastor in her area. The

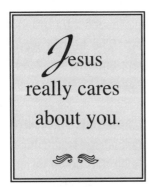

love and compassion she received from God's people during this difficult time greatly encouraged her. "That following Sunday, I began going to church. When my Christian father-in-law looked up, he was very surprised to see me there. He had been praying for our family!" she exclaims.

God has done amazing things in response to prayer. "During those rough times when I didn't know which way things were going to go, Psalm 46:10 kept coming into my mind: *'Be still, and know that I am God....'* I wrote down that verse and put it on my fridge. Seven months later, the Lord reconciled our marriage and our family." And Michelle has discovered that having her family together again is one of the greatest blessings! —KS

❧ *85* ❧

Susan Aglukark

Northern Light

As she made her way to the podium to accept the Juno prize for Best Aboriginal Canada Recording and Best New Solo Artist for her *Arctic Rose* album, Susan Aglukark smiled. She had come a long way from her home in Eskimo Point.

Born and raised in the Arctic, Susan loved to sit and write poetry. At the age of nine, she began singing in the church her father pastored, which was located in a small, isolated community on the west coast of Hudson's Bay. A natural performer, before long, she was writing her own songs.

One day, at the age of 11, Susan was at home with her mother listening to a gospel album. Although she had heard the salvation message over and over again, this time it pierced her heart. She began to cry – not tears of sorrow or pain, but tears of love. Sensitive to what the Holy Spirit was doing in her daughter's life, Susan's mother did not need an explanation for the tears. Together, they prayed and sensed an incredible presence of the Holy Spirit in the room.

High school presented challenges unfamiliar to Susan. Her friends began to harass her because of her stand for Christ. Rather than pull her away from her faith, however, the experience solidified her commitment and she started up a Christian youth group.

In 1990, Susan made her way to Ottawa, where she continued to pursue her love for music. As recognition grew through her personal appearances, she became a role model for the youth. Her popular educational video, *Searching*, won the Top

Cinematography Award from *MuchMusic*. Her first recording, *Dreams for You*, received extensive airplay across the Arctic.

In 1993, described by the president of Inuit Tapirisat of Canada as "an ambassador for the Inuits, a woman of wisdom, a leader," she was chosen as one of the *100 Leaders to Watch For* by *MacLean's* magazine. That same year, the Northwest Territories publication, *Up Here*, named her 1993 Northerner of the Year. Thus the door was open for her to represent the Canadian Inuits at the World Conference on Human Rights in Vienna and at the Davvi Suuva Music Festival in Sweden.

Having been a victim of sexual abuse when she was a child, Susan feels that she has been given a unique opportunity to speak out on social issues such as teen suicide, drugs and alcohol. Rather than carrying a bold message of the Gospel during her concerts, she simply encourages people to love one another and stop criticizing others. At the end of the concerts, she is often asked how she handled her own abuse, at which time she shares her faith in Jesus, assuring listeners that He can heal the pain and wounds in their lives.

> *A*lthough Susan had heard the salvation message over and over again, this time it pierced her heart.

Susan's music carries a vision for the fulfillment of hopes and dreams, and leads listeners to search for meaning in their own lives. —DRL

Forgive the abuser. With the Lord, you can forgive anything.

≫ *86* ≈

Harold Short

Beyond Death's Door

"When I grow up, Dad, I want to be just like you – get big like you, have a moustache and smoke cigarettes!"

Harold Short can still remember hearing these words, spoken years ago by his son Jeff, who was then only six years old. However, thinking back on those earlier days, Harold now realizes that he was not the best role model for his three children. "I would use the Lord's Name in vain and was a heavy smoker," he states. "At the time, I was smoking up to three packs of cigarettes a day.

Despite all his efforts, he couldn't stop this addictive habit which had such a hold on his life. In fact, every time he tried to quit, he was unbearable to be around. "He wasn't fit to live with," teasingly quips his wife Mildred.

When Mildred became a Christian, Harold only got more and more agitated. "Actually, I used to give her a hard time," he says. "I was bitter and didn't want anything to do with church or the Gospel in any way. I wouldn't even allow her to play Christian music in the house. I told her that if she played any more Christian music, I would destroy it."

Circumstances made it very difficult for Mildred and her three young children to attend church regularly. So in order to receive spiritual nourishment and growth, she considered her mother-in-law's suggestion to watch *100 Huntley Street*. Harold explains how this had an impact on him too: "Mildred began to watch the program regularly and started to support the Crossroads Ministry. During that time, Crossroads offered a book written by Dr. Maurice Rawlings entitled, *Beyond Death's Door*" (Dr. Rawlings' testimony, page 21).

An avid reader, Harold read the book in a short period of time. The reality of heaven and hell made him assess the destiny of his own life. "I have a very vivid imagination. As Dr. Rawlings was describing the events of several patients who testified of their near death experiences, it was real in my mind. Although I didn't know it, I was under conviction," he adds.

Within days of reading the incredible accounts of life after death, Harold decided to go to church. When he mentioned this to Mildred, she was shocked that this same man – the one who was so opposed to Christianity, and even the mere suggestion of church – could have such a drastic change of heart.

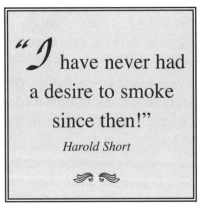

> "*I* have never had a desire to smoke since then!"
>
> *Harold Short*

That Sunday evening, Harold was once again under the heavy conviction of the Holy Spirit. "When I went to church," he recalls, "the pastor preached along the same lines. Suddenly, I again began to visualize all that Dr. Rawlings had described in his book."

On March 2, 1980, Harold gave his life – and his smoking habit – over to the Lord. He says, "That same night I got saved, I requested prayer for the Lord to deliver me from smoking. The Lord delivered me instantly that night and I have never had a desire to smoke since then!"

By the way, when Harold's family began attending church together, Jeff also changed his life's goal. Yes, he still wanted to get big and have a moustache like his dad... except this time (instead of smoking), he wanted to go to heaven! —KS

～ 87 ～

Andrew & Louisa Weistch

"For I am the Lord who heals you." Exodus 15:26

Andrew and Louisa Weistch were in crisis. On top of their marital problems, Andrew was suicidal. Louisa was desperate.

Alcohol was a major problem on their reserve in northern Quebec. Two weeks before the Christmas of 1979, Andrew's best friend had committed suicide after drinking the three bottles of liquor Andrew had given him. Andrew was inconsolable. What was he supposed to do after the suicide of his best friend? Searching for an answer, he and Louisa ended up at church the day after Christmas. Hope stirred within Andrew as he listened to the message. As the Holy Spirit began to fill them both with an awesome sense of the love of Jesus, Louisa walked with him to the front of the church and they responded to His call.

Andrew is sure that, had Jesus not given him a reason to live that day, he probably would have committed suicide as did his friend.

But that was only the beginning of God's work in the lives of Andrew and Louisa. In 1990, Louisa was diagnosed with chronic leukemia. According to the prognosis, she had no hope of living longer than two years without chemotherapy, radiation and a bone marrow transplant. As soon as she heard the diagnosis, Louisa knew that God would heal her. Despite the fact that she appeared to deteriorate, she never lost her faith and encouraged Andrew to trust God.

Things didn't look good. At one point, Louisa had a seizure and died in the hospital. Completely aware of the experience, she saw her body lying on the bed with the doctors and nurses surrounding her. Suddenly, she knew that she was being escorted to heaven. As the heavenly city came into view, the colours and reflections were more beautiful than any human words could describe. Then came the majestic voice of God, telling her that her time on earth was not yet over and she needed to return to finish her work for Him. Although longing to stay, she returned to her body.

About a week before Christmas, a transplant donor was found and Louisa was admitted to the Montreal General Hospital. For some reason, God allowed her to experience the loss of her hair and the excruciating pain of the procedures. Andrew's response to Louisa's ordeal was to cut off his braids and shave his head as a symbol of his love for her. Throughout it all, Psalm 46:1 stuck in their heads: *"God is our refuge and strength, a very present help in trouble."*

For a year, Louisa underwent weekly treatments and then suffered another setback, this time so severe that the doctors told Andrew that she would most likely die. They warned that if she were to live, she would be bedridden for the rest of her life.

For Andrew, this was the darkest hour of his Christian life. The thought of losing his wife, the mother of their seven children, was just too much to bear. At the blackest moment, just as it seemed that all hope was gone, Jesus came to the rescue, saying, *"For I am the Lord who heals you"* (Exodus 15:26). The Word of the Lord was powerful and true. Louisa was healed.

With a clean bill of health, she left the hospital at her husband's side. Today, Andrew is a pastor/teacher, responsible for the local Spirit-filled Cree church. Wherever the doors open, he travels to other reserves to preach the Gospel, always sharing the story of God's mercy to his family. —DRL

The grace of God is very present for the person in trouble. God gives peace.

✺ 88 ✺

Nancy Delaney

Basking in the "Sonshine" of God's Love

The quest for happiness gradually led Nancy Delaney on a spiral descent of destruction. Her heavy involvement in the occult, along with the abuse of alcohol and drugs, only left her more confused and in a dark state of depression.

It all began very innocently when she was a teenager and oblivious to the dangers of the occult. Disillusioned by the cold formality of the church she attended as a child, Nancy initially tried to fill the spiritual void in her life with horoscopes (astrology), tarot cards, palmistry and New Age teaching. Eventually, she progressed deeper into the occult and the resulting destructive consequences of demonic activity:

"While at college, I met a man who was a sorcerer. It seemed to me he had the answers and power that I was needing in my life. I started practising witchcraft, black magic, psychometry, numerology, past-life regression and different types of meditation...."

The dark side of the spiritual realm became more obvious to Nancy when she began the practice of channelling (writing or speaking on behalf of the spirit guides). "It was very real and frightening," she admits. "I now realize that the enemy was trying to destroy me, and he was doing a good job."

In 1992, Nancy reached a point of sheer desperation. "I lost my job, my heart was broken due to the breakup of a relationship and I had to have surgery," she explains. "I went into a really deep depression, and channelling didn't bring me any comfort. And although there were people in my life, I felt very much alone."

With the TV on in the background, Nancy paced the floor restlessly. Because of the demonic activity in her life, she felt a repulsion toward Christianity and couldn't even utter the Name of Jesus. There was a strong struggle within her every time she felt drawn toward the things of God. It was during this time of difficulty and confusion that she began to watch *100 Huntley Street* intermittently:

"I recall David Mainse inviting anyone who needed prayer to call the number on the bottom of the screen. The prayer partner I spoke to was very loving and her manner was peaceful. I was so blessed when she prayed for me. She seemed to zoom right in on all the needs I had."

Through the ongoing ministry of *100 Huntley Street* and the implementation of the 12-step program, Nancy felt as if she was slowly being brought out of the pit of destruction. As the Lord began to move in her life, He revealed the need for her to belong to a good church family. Upon the recommendation of the Crossroads Ministry Centre, she found a vibrant church in her area.

Nancy remembers being overwhelmed by the warmth and love she received when she entered the church building. "They are an amazingly loving group of people," she acknowledges. "They really demonstrate the love of Jesus!"

With the wise guidance and spiritual discernment of her pastor, she came to understand the importance of renouncing in prayer all former occult activity. Then following the Lord's leading, she collected everything in her home that was associated with the occult. One by one, she placed these items in the wood stove to be destroyed while pleading the blood of Jesus and rebuking every evil thing related to them.

Because of all the Lord has done in her life, Nancy feels like a brand new person today. With heartfelt gratitude she says, "I have such peace and joy.... The fear I used to have is gone. There is so much love in my life now that I can't explain it in words. It is beyond what I ever imagined!" —KS

✍ 89 ✍

𝒫at & 𝒯om 𝒞olwell

Two Shall Become as One

"Happy ever after" was hardly the way the Colwell marriage appeared to be working out. With their firstborn son followed by twins, the seven years since their 1964 marriage had been a confusing time of inadequacy in meeting each other's needs. Neither had any idea of how to find that place of appreciative, loving response from the other.

Believing that marriage required her to unconditionally support her husband without ever criticizing him, Pat was totally unprepared to cope with the irresponsibility Tom had developed from his dysfunctional upbringing. Having been shown no love in his home, Tom believed that it was a man's place to conquer situations rather than contribute positively to their success. In place of genuine love, all he had to offer was selfish manipulation.

For seven years, Pat endured the façade. However, with the children finally all in school, she left the marriage, went to university and became a teacher. Having been raised in a religious home where tradition masqueraded as relationship, she felt that because she was unable to follow the church rules, she couldn't talk to God. Believing herself to be cut off from her greatest source of wisdom and strength, her faith floundered. After a few years of living unsatisfied with the ways of the world, she listened as her brother showed her the way to salvation. She gave her heart to Jesus and her life began to turn around.

Meanwhile, Tom spent the 14 years following the separation driven by fear. Success always eluded him and alcohol became his most constant companion.

Finally, in 1983, while leafing through his local newspaper, he saw an ad for a Focus on the Family presentation. He went to the meeting and left with a craving to have his family back. All he wanted to do was go home and restore his family to God's will. He called Pat that night, the beginning of a three-year platonic relationship in which he began to rebuild relationships with his wife and children.

One night, he went home drunk, evidence that there had really been no inner change. As he looked into the pain and disappointment in the eyes of his family, he realized that he needed help. The next day, he went into the Brentwood Recovery Home and began attending church.

In the spring of 1984, the church hosted the *Heaven's Gates – Hell's Flames* theatre production. As Tom watched the dramatized everyday events unfold into eternal significance, the frailty of his life and situation was suddenly so clear. He recommitted his life to Christ and was baptized.

Anxious to get his life back on track, Tom asked Pat whether they could get back together. Still recognizing the stubborn selfishness in him, however, she refused. She could see that he had not yet really made Jesus Lord in his life and knew that they would never make it a second time unless Tom were to relinquish control of his life to God.

At the end of himself, Tom went home and cried out to God. There the Lord met him in that precious place of total surrender. Drinking had been only a symptom. Now he was ready to truly have his mind transformed. As he began to read the New Testament, the Word became alive in his heart. Now God was changing him from the inside out.

One month later, Tom's phone rang. It was Pat. She had called to tell him that she felt they should get married again! From the time of his initial return into her life, it had taken her three years to forgive him, but now she was ready to begin again!

With a deep desire to share the precious wisdom he had found, Tom eventually became the director of Brentwood, the recovery home for alcohol and substance abusers where he, himself, went for help in 1983. He is now the director of Parkwood Counselling Centre. —DRL

God gives wisdom. However, we must: 1) admit that we need it, 2) decide that we want it, and 3) commit ourselves to obeying His direction.

≈ 90 ≈

Abe Plett

A Prodigal Comes Home

The surroundings of the prison aptly convey the bleakness and emptiness of such an existence. And although 17-year-old Abe Plett was only incarcerated for a brief period of time for a minor misdemeanor, it didn't quench his yearning for life in the fast lane.

During his many years of rebellion, Abe somehow knew that God had never left him nor forsaken him. He attributes this to the Christian upbringing he received as a child. "When I got older though," he admits, "I felt that God didn't want me to have any fun. So in order to have fun, I turned my back on my Christian upbringing. But my dad was always very strong in the Word, strong in prayer and strong in faith."

With hindsight, Abe can now see that God's hand was on him throughout the years, even in his state of rebellion. "The

Lord's protection was on my life," he adds. "He kept me from death and destruction many times."

One particular event took place on July 3, 1967, when Abe and his wife Judy were involved in a tragic car accident that almost claimed their lives: "I suggested we go to the bar for a few drinks with another couple. Judy agreed only on the condition that I didn't drive as I had already been drinking that day. On the way home, the driver decided to show us how fast his car could go. He accelerated to a high speed and lost control of the car...."

At the scene of the accident, it was noted that Abe and Judy had been thrown out of the vehicle. Witnesses carefully carried Judy, who was lying in gasoline, safely to the side of the road. However, when the ambulance attendants came over to check Abe's vital signs, he had none. "I was taken to the hospital to be declared dead." he states. "The Lord, of course, had other plans. Half way to the hospital, I began thrashing around in the back of the ambulance, requiring them to tie me down."

During the next several months, Judy and Abe miraculously recovered in spite of the life-threatening prognoses they both received. Yet the process proved to be an arduous and extremely painful ordeal. "Most people think this would have been enough to turn my heart back to the Lord," Abe confides. "But in my stubbornness, it didn't. I went back to my old lifestyle of drinking and partying and doing whatever I wanted."

It wasn't until 17 years later, in November of '84, that Abe finally paid attention to what God was trying to tell him: "I listened as a man testified on *100 Huntley Street* of how God had spared him from death and destruction so many times.... At the close of his testimony, he said to those who had walked away from God, 'Now is the time to invite the Lord back into your life!'

"As I listened to him, I thought, 'Yes, Lord, it's time. It's time I came home. It's time the prodigal son came back!' And from that moment on, I made a regular point of watching *100 Huntley Street*. I found it astonishing how God orchestrated it all. He knew that this testimony was exactly what I needed to hear to touch my life and draw me back."

Ironically, Abe now goes into the prison on a regular basis. However, this time he ministers to inmates – testifying of God's mercy and grace. "The Lord is no respecter of persons," he says. "He will do the same for others as He has done for me. And He has certainly done many great and wondrous things!" —KS

～ *91* ～

₱at & Elaine O'Rourke

"The Lord gave and the Lord has taken away;
blessed be the Name of the Lord." Job 1:21

Late one afternoon, Pat went for a walk. As the pastor of a busy church, he was taking advantage of some scheduled quiet time during their church retreat. With every step on the forested path, he luxuriated in the beauty of his Master's creation.

The screams of children suddenly shook Pat from his reverie. Running towards the sounds of panic, he could see his ten-year-old daughter Grace stuck in a big hole. With sudden horror, he realized that it was a bear's den! As she struggled in abject terror, his beloved Grace was being pulled in, feet first, by a 300-pound black bear!

With no thought but the immediate extrication of his precious little girl, Pat jumped into the hole, furiously kicking at the rock-hard head of the bear. For 25 minutes, the father and the bear struggled for possession of the precious child.

As Grace finally died with the Name of Jesus on her lips, she remained still firmly held in the jaws of the bear. Pat, too, continued to hold her. As others arrived with efforts to assist, the bear turned on Pat, grinding its powerful teeth into the bones of his leg, all the while shaking its massive head. Having pulled out a fence post, one man gave the predator a great blow, freeing Pat. Still the enraged beast continued its attack. Finally someone arrived with a gun and the great beast slumped into silence.

From the moment when Pat's wife Elaine first saw her mauled daughter, she knew that she was dead. There was no question in her mind. With the unexplainable explosion of joy that suddenly surged in her heart, she saw the beauty that God had seen in His Son as He had hung on the cross. Contrary to the expectations of those who thought that Elaine's response was symptomatic of shock, the joy never left her.

For six weeks following his heroic struggle to save his little girl, Pat lay in the hospital, initially drifting in and out of consciousness. He remained under the threat of losing his leg. Five days after his admission, he had a vision of heaven which opened his understanding of victorious Christian living as gaining triumph over tragedy through worship. This sustained him through the days and months which followed. Also critical to Pat and Elaine in the entire process was the reality of the body of Christ surrounding them. Everyone involved gave of themselves in remarkable ways.

As the days passed, Elaine remembered a sermon and a piece of Scripture which, at the time, had meant little to her. The Scripture was Hebrews 10:34: *"You cheerfully accepted the seizure of your possessions"* (NEB). Now she understood that God gives us joy, but it is our choice whether or not we keep it. What seizure or robbery could be more painful than that of a child? Elaine realized that God had been preparing her for what lay ahead and that He was all she really needed. He told her to continue to rejoice through those awful months. As she held on to her joy, it was so explosive within her that she sometimes could hardly contain it – a result of responding to God rather than reacting to a death in her family.

Grateful for His sustaining love, even in the worst possible circumstance life could present, Pat and Elaine have learned to trust God moment by moment for their lives. —DRL

Honour what the Lord has done for you and receive it. There is nothing going on in this world that is not under the authority of God. What we suffer now is nothing compared to the glory we will receive later with Him.

≫ *92* ≈

Deborah Klassen

True To His Word

"They tell me when I was three, I was so shy that I hid inside the pulpit while I sang," says the Juno Award winner Deborah Klassen. Travelling with her family, ministering at different churches, Deborah has been singing all her life.

On one of the trips, she met Earl. He was 17, she not quite 14. After four years of letter writing, phoning and visiting periodically, Earl decided to ask Deb's parents if they could get married. "When I entered into this marriage, I expected Earl to be everything I needed and to solve all my problems."

In reality, Deborah and Earl were two deeply wounded people. "Earl worked all the time. That was his means of value and security. Two years later Ryan was born." Eighteen months after that, all the pain caved in. "I really wanted to take my life and exit," admits Deborah. "I felt like such a disappointment to God, drowning in pain. Our marriage was broken. And so I checked myself into a psychiatric hospital in Guelph."

At 21, Deborah hit rock bottom. "But Jesus pursued me," she adds. "I have come to realize that God's love for us has been there long before time. If I try to hide in the darkness, even the darkness is light unto Him. He knows everything about me. In that place of real imprisonment, I ended up on my face before God, repenting of trying to be my *own* "saviour" and asking Him to be Lord."

And He became the Rock. When Ryan was seven and had spinal meningitis, God brought him through. Then, three years later, he was diagnosed with a tumour in his right nostril. "We stopped the aggressive chemotherapy after 18 months," she says, "because Ryan reacted adversely. It was killing him."

"A couple of years ago, one of the top doctors in Canada said to me: 'Deb, I could show you the stats on survivors. I dare say that Ryan's survival has more to do with the healing touch of Jesus Christ than medicine.'"

As Ryan was left disfigured, he underwent a number of surgeries. "When they finished the last surgery they said there is nothing more they can do because two thirds of his nostril room didn't grow. He is working through a lot of stuff. But God cares, for we are His. And what He ordains, He holds to. The Word says that nobody and nothing can take us out of His hand. We wept and cried unto God. And He opened a door of hope. Ryan met a doctor who is going to be working with him."

"As I continue on in this journey of life, I continue to learn. Earl lost his kidney to cancer a couple of years ago. We continue to learn that God is faithful. When all the circumstances and events of life scream in your face to the contrary, He is faithful and true to His Word." —HS

✨ *93* ✨

Marie Clausen

Rape is Not Just a Four-Letter Word

Accepting the Lord into one's heart does not come with a ticket to free parking in this life. Christians, like non-Christians, are subject to painful circumstances. The difference is whether they are given to God as tools for a deeper work within – or retained to destroy the bearer with fear and bitterness.

In 1969, Marie Clausen walked forward to publicly accept Jesus at a *Billy Graham Crusade*. Although she always believed that Jesus was God's Son and that He died on the cross as a substitute for her, she had never been willing to publicly proclaim Him until that moment – the beginning of her spiritual journey.

Twenty years later, at just over 40 years of age, she was watching TV one afternoon. "If you're a woman watching this show with two other women," the broadcaster began, "statistics indicate that one of the three of you will be assaulted in your lifetime." Marie vaguely thought that it would never happen to her.

That night, returning home from choir practice, she was tired. Following her usual nightly ritual, she turned out the lights and went to bed. Hearing a strange clanking noise, her parakeet began thrashing around in its cage. Marie got out of bed, but before she could switch on a light, she was attacked and thrown back on her bed by an intruder in dark clothing. Wrapping long, bony fingers around her throat, the stranger choked her until she could no longer scream or breathe. Just as she began to lose consciousness, he released his grip and unzipped his pants.

Initially, Marie cried out to Jesus for help, hoping for instant deliverance, but the invader seemed not to notice. Then, praying silently for peace and wisdom, an incomprehensible calm enveloped her. Almost immediately, she began to memorize details about the man – his size, his voice, his smell.

After 45 minutes of what seemed to be interminable brutality, the assailant stole away, leaving Marie bound, gagged and handcuffed. Somehow managing to call 911, she huddled beside her bed, sobbing uncontrollably until the police arrived four minutes later.

Then came the long road to recovery, over and over again replaying the tapes in her mind as she shared every disgusting detail with dear friends whose compassion and willingness to listen, talk and cry with her sped up the healing process.

Nine days after the rape, determined to go on with her life, Marie steeled herself to return to her apartment. Week by week, she began to increasingly relax and turn out the lights at night.

When people ask whether she ever questions why God allowed this to happen to her, she replies, "No." She considers herself a victor because she learned to go on living. She did not allow the rapist to alter her life forever. Although it wasn't easy and took a great deal of time and prayer, Marie realizes that nothing could have changed what happened. She chose to focus on God's blessings and mercies, allowing Jesus to remove her fear and pain. Now she says, "It's as though it never happened!" —DRL

> *She* chose to focus on God's blessings and mercies, allowing Jesus to remove her fear and pain.

A dead spirit tied to your mind and body, suffering from guilt, emptiness and loneliness will destroy you. You'll never have peace of mind until your spirit comes alive.

❧ 94 ❧

Desmond Wall

A Lonely Wanderer Finds the Way

With one hand raised high in the air, the floor director motions the countdown. Five, four, three, two, one. The light on one of the large state-of-the-art cameras gives the signal and the musician begins playing his guitar. In praise to God and as a tribute of gratitude to *100 Huntley Street,* Desmond Wall sings, "Feeling lonely, my heart was broken and no one to call my friend. And then the Light shone in the darkness of my heart and I was overcome with joy...."

For Desmond, performing his testimonial, *A Love Song,* on *100 Huntley Street* was of great significance, for it recaptured the day he fully surrendered his life to God. "Back in 1985, I was backslidden and far away from the Lord," he explains. "I was also unemployed and depressed. I began flipping through the channels on my TV. Then I saw David Mainse exhorting the TV audience to recommit their lives to Jesus. It felt like he was talking directly to me. Right there and then, I made that recommitment in prayer, and I haven't looked back."

Prior to tuning in to *100 Huntley Street,* Desmond spent many years wandering aimlessly. Whether on the streets of Toronto, California, or even Amsterdam, the deception of drug use kept luring him in the wrong direction.

Succumbing to the temptation only increased his feelings of loneliness. "As a teenager, I experimented with drugs and alcohol. This continued for 15 years. I decided that I needed to get away." Getting away meant moving to Amsterdam for awhile. However, Desmond soon realized that he couldn't get away from the pull of the city's legalized hashish bars – nor could he get away from God's sovereign grace.

"I had been to Amsterdam a couple of times before as a traveller and decided to settle down there because I really loved Holland. While wandering down the streets of Amsterdam, I came upon the Christian youth hostel called 'The Shelter.'"

It was there Desmond was first introduced to Jesus. Although he wasn't well-grounded spiritually, support came in the form of a TV screen: "*100 Huntley Street* had a major part in turning my life around. It was the first step in a long process of getting me back to where God wanted me to be – firmly planted in His kingdom."

Quietly strumming his guitar, Desmond reflects on God's goodness in his life: "The Lord has really blessed me. I have a lovely wife and five young children. If it wasn't for *100 Huntley Street,* I probably wouldn't be serving the Lord today. In fact, I would probably be still wandering aimlessly. God really does change lives – He changed mine!" —KS

↬ 95 ↫

Darka Nazarko

The Heart of Magdalene

Darka Nazarko had long ago locked herself up in a black box within. Suicide haunted the thoughts pressing in on all sides, threatening to break into the box and steal her life.

She had been a heroin addict for nearly 20 years. Dealing to support her habit, she had been arrested many times and had spent long, agonizingly hopeless days in jail.

Darka knew all about God. As a pretty little girl in pony tails, she had gone to Sunday school and learned all about Jesus. She had learned so much that even with the choices she eventually made, she could still debate His reality as the Son of God – but had never accepted Him personally.

In 1975, when on the run from the police, she went to the home of an old friend. While there, the friend persuaded Darka to accompany her to church. With the warmth of the sanctuary lights, the security of the familiar old hymns, and a promise of salvation, Darka responded to the altar call and accepted Jesus. However, still on the lam, she had to leave her friend's house with no follow-up.

Life got worse. Prostitution seemed the only way to get the money she needed for her drugs. With her soul jammed into the black box inside, she did things to her body that God never intended. He must have wept over the emptiness of her broken-ness – but He never let her go. Even in the darkest of circum-stances, He was there with questions that loomed large in her mind: "What was her purpose for living? Whose pawn was she?"

Having decided to go south, she met a little boy who was selling books of poems. They spoke of Jesus and Darka bought one. Leafing through the verses, they gave a solace to her soul that no drug could sustain.

Two months later, returning to Toronto, she began to watch *The 700 Club* and *100 Huntley Street*, feeling that they gave her protection from the demons while she did her drugs. But the message began to penetrate the drug fog: Jesus could change her life. One day, Darka got down on one knee and asked Jesus to get her off the drugs and change her life.

And He did! Gone are the drugs, the street life and the hard music. Now, no longer searching for her purpose in life, she is filled with peace and contentment. Having enrolled in college, Darka is taking counselling courses and is very involved in missions and her church. With the goal of obtaining a counselling degree from a Christian college, the rubber meets the road with her volunteer work on city streets through the Salvation Army and her church's outreach. —DRL

I stand in awe at God's love for me. I long for a deeper walk - intimacy with God.

✖ 96 ✖

Bruce Marchiano

In the Footsteps of Jesus

His history professor once told him, "Bruce, God has something big planned for your life. I don't know what it is, but it's really, really big."

Actor Bruce Marchiano grew up in southern California. At age 13, he played his first role in a high school production of Oliver. His first professional gig came in 1984, a brief walk-on which consisted of three lines for the show, *Murder, She Wrote*. "Well, as wonderful as that first acting job was, it would only launch me into several years of struggle," Bruce states.

In 1987, Bruce met the girl of his dreams. By that time his career was taking on a nice pace. "I was having the time of my life!" he says. But his dream eventually came crashing down one hot July evening. Disappointed, he started to search for answers. He recollects how this spiritual journey brought him to a point of total surrender: "One July afternoon, in the park in the hills, I gave my life to Jesus. Praise His Holy Name!"

With a desire to honour God with his life and future, Bruce's career really took off. "I believe it was the Lord making sure I knew that He was very real and very interested in me. As I dove into the Word and nestled into a great church, I began to grow."

The young actor began to grow spiritually, and so did the opportunities to minister to audiences through drama. In 1991, Bruce joined a drama ministry that was travelling to Australia. "When I returned from the tour, my agent dropped me, saying, 'Bruce, this Christian thing is getting in the way.'" Struggling again, Bruce clung to his faith.

One day the phone rang. It was Jerry Fisher, the drama ministry leader. "A South African director is making a new Jesus movie," he told Bruce. "He's looking for a more down-to-earth, more real-looking Jesus, a professional actor who's born again. I think you might be right for this."

Without hesitation, Bruce was in contact with the director. "The next thing I knew, I had a beard and long hair, and was on a plane to Morocco to play the role of a lifetime – the Son of the Living God made Man – JESUS!!!!"

The scene of Jesus' crucifixion proved to be much more difficult than he anticipated: "It was gruelling in every way – physically, emotionally, and I have to believe, spiritually. I will never forget the mutilation I felt in my face, the hell of being tossed and kicked around. I will never forget hanging from that crossbeam and counting the seconds till they took me down. It was terrible beyond description. Jesus, and what He did for the likes of me!

"Now, years later, I continue to share Jesus as I discovered Him, as an actor. I've seen thousands give their lives to Jesus. Every time I stand in front of an audience, every time I hold a child in Africa, every time I walk by a book rack and see my name under 'written by,' every time a flight attendant says, 'Aren't you the guy who played Jesus?'...I stand amazed, stunned, astounded. He is good, and He is God." —HS

✎ *97* ✎

Martin & Catherine Bennett

Alpha to Omega

Martin was brought up in the church, but thought of God simply as something one might come across after death. As he progressed into his teen years, he became very anti-God, anti-Jesus, anti-church and anti-religion. Understandably.

At the age of 12, he was abused by a teacher, a very high pro-file man in the church. An alcoholic, the teacher introduced Martin to Scotch and vodka, got him very drunk and then took criminal liberties with him. Enlisting Martin's confidence, he warned him that everything they did had to be kept totally secret or they would both be in great trouble. Binding him in secrecy, the teacher established an emotional bond that Martin had never wanted. He handled it by completely switching his emotions off.

Throughout Martin's teen years, the teacher bedeviled him by fabricating reasons for meetings every time he would attempt to break free of his hold over him. The whole cycle would recommence, and once again, Martin would be forced into covering the tracks of his double life.

Martin's parents had no idea what was happening to their son. As far as they were concerned, the teacher was a fine, upstanding member of the community and any time Martin spent with him should be a time of positive role modelling. Little did they know that their son was quickly becoming an alcoholic. Drinking to make things easier and to try to forget his problems, his hospitalization with acute pancreatitis at age 20 developed complications when the doctor prescribed drugs that could not be used in conjunction with alcohol.

At age 26, the abuse, the alcoholism, the drug conflicts and the deception all came to a head. Martin's girlfriend, Catherine, knew something was very wrong. Thus began the rounds of psychiatrists, psychologists, psychoanalysts, and psychotherapists. Some were okay, some were awful, some were useless. None relieved his guilt, pain and shame.

Admitted to a detox centre for the alcoholism, Martin finally began to talk about the abuse. Not wanting to make a big issue of it in the community, and yet feeling the responsibility of not leaving other children vulnerable to the teacher, Martin cooperated to the point of ensuring that the man would never teach again.

Martin and Catherine were married in 1992. That year, Catherine began to attend an Alpha course in the church. Very excited about what she was learning, she soon learned not to mention it to Martin because of the predictable arguments that would ensue. From time to time, however, she would ask him to go to a meeting with her.

Finally, noticing a distinct change in his wife, Martin decided to check Alpha out to determine where she was getting her inner peace. After a few visits to the church during which he experienced an unexplainable depth of response, he decided to have a talk with the Alpha course leader, Nicky Gumbel. Following their initial greeting, Nicky said, "So, Martin, tell me a little bit about yourself."

As Martin began, the whole story began to emerge in frank detail – something that had never before happened with any of the horde of doctors he had visited. When he finished, he agreed to follow Nicky in prayer to ask God to come into his life. In the process of praying, Nicky urged Martin to forgive the teacher for what he had done to him. With forgiveness being a totally foreign concept, Martin attempted to do it three times. Each time he spoke the words, the burden got a little lighter. By the third time, he felt an incredible release of the weight that had dragged him down for so long. The total cleansing accomplished by Jesus was so far ahead of anything any of the doctors ever attempted to do that there was no comparison. When Martin arrived home, Catherine was thrilled.

The following Sunday, when the invitation for the infilling of the Holy Spirit was given, Martin responded and experienced a rush of the Holy Spirit throughout his entire being, strengthening him to live the Christian life.

Awhile ago, Martin and Catherine looked back over her prayer diary from those days. It has entries like: "Prayed that Martin does go to church," Tick. "Prayed that Martin does the Alpha course." Tick. "Prayed that Martin becomes a Christian." Big tick with a smiley face! —DRL

There is a power beyond all psychiatry or medicine. "It is the Spirit who gives life; the flesh profits nothing. The words that I speak to you are spirit, and they are life" (John 6:63).

✽ 98 ✽
Deborah Dissler

Hope at the Brink

The year was 1978. It was a cold November night and Deborah Dissler had given up. She was preparing to end her life. It would finally put a stop to the pain and emptiness that had plagued her 28 years of existence....

Deborah, the youngest of three children, always felt alone as a child – like she didn't fit in. As a vulnerable teenager looking for love, she become involved with a young man and soon found herself pregnant. Deborah's shameful situation was hushed as she was sent off to a home for unwed mothers in Chicago. There she had her child and reluctantly gave it up for adoption. Deborah returned home to complete grade 12, and she felt more alienated than ever.

After high school, Deborah went off on her own back to Chicago to look for a career. A whirlwind romance and four-month marriage landed her back into depression and loneliness. An acquaintance from San Francisco suggested she move out there, and in her search to fill her emptiness, she packed up and went. It was the early '70s, and the "hippie" culture was in full swing. Soon Deborah was right in the thick of it, complete with the parties, drugs and Eastern philosophy.

Deborah then met her second husband, and one week after their marriage, he told her that he felt they had made a mistake. Though devastated, she wanted to keep the relationship together. Three moves and one baby boy later, they decided to move to Canada.

Deborah felt that this move represented their last chance at making the marriage work. They packed everything they owned into their "hippie" van, and with $200 and a 10-month-old, they headed for British Columbia.

They ended up in a tiny bush village near Prince George with a total population of about 100, including cats and dogs. However, a series of circumstances convinced Deborah to take her son and leave. Then she met Glenn. He seemed to be everything she ever wanted, so as was the "hippie" thing to do, she moved in with him. Within two weeks, she was pregnant with twins, and less than two years after their birth, along came number four.

Difficult times forced Deborah, Glenn and the children to move to the city in search of stable employment. The pressures of mothering, combined with her life-long emotional pain and emptiness, finally plunged Deborah into a pit of depression she couldn't escape. It was then she began to convince herself she'd be better off dead.

> "*W*elcome to the family of God!"
>
> *David Mainse*

All this led up to that November night in 1978 when Deborah decided to end it all. Before she carried out the rest of her plan, however, she turned on the television. They only received two channels, and on one was *100 Huntley Street*. David Mainse and his team were broadcasting a local stewardship telethon.

Deborah began mocking and swearing at them. But as she listened to various testimonies of everyday people whose lives had been changed by the power of Christ, her heart began to soften. She longed for that same kind of miracle to happen in her life. Deborah sensed God saying to her, "You're ready to give your life up anyway, so why don't you let Me have a go at it?" And she did! That night she invited Jesus into her life.

When Deborah finally gathered the nerve to call the prayer line to report her decision, the program was already over. David Mainse answered the phone. When she explained what she had done, David's reply was, "Welcome to the family of God!" After a short conversation, he took her name and number and a church soon got in touch with her.

Things have never been the same for Deborah, Glenn (now her husband) and their four children. God has changed the course of their lives and continues to minister hope and healing in their family. —RM

∽ 99 ∾

Jerry Howarth

Voice of the Blue Jays

With the best seat in the house for watching major league baseball, Jerry Howarth loves his work as a play-by-play broadcaster for the Toronto Blue Jays.

Growing up playing baseball year round just north of San Francisco, Jerry had no thoughts of a broadcasting career. Needing a small college where he could find himself following his parents' divorce, he picked Santa Clara University. He now says it was the best thing that ever happened to him spiritually. Besides his dad's influence, three people helped him get a glimpse of God: "John Shanks told us to love, praise, and serve the Lord and our careers would follow. Austin Fagothey showed me that a life of discipline and routine would bring rewards and satisfaction. Tom Brogan, our all-American first baseman of '66, taught me how to listen to God."

Following two years in the army and a year in law school, Jerry took a leave of absence for a year to see if he could take his passion for sports and turn it into a career.

Going back to his alma mater, Santa Clara University, Jerry joined the athletic department. To hone his announcing skills, he purchased a tape recorder and practised play-by-play of Santa Clara football and basketball. Beginning his way up the ladder by moving to Tacoma, his career really began at the University of Puget Sound in 1973, with a football game between "the Sound" and Slippery Rock. Following a variety of announcing jobs, he joined the Blue Jays in 1982, a job he feels incredibly blessed and fortunate to have.

In 1985, despite the success and blessings of his life, he knew that something was missing. Even though he had recognized the value of the spiritual influence gained in his college years, Jerry had not accepted Christ into his life.

That same year, Jerry got to know Gary Lavelle, one of baseball's top relief pitchers. Gary's life radiated real joy and peace. He had a way of communicating a wealth of Scripture without overwhelming those in his presence. Although Jerry had gone to church for many years, he had never read the Bible. Gary and Tony Kubek, a TV broadcaster, encouraged him to pick up the NIV Bible, a translation that was easy to read and understand, thus demystifying the Book from which Jerry had shied away.

The two men helped Jerry to understand the importance of getting to know God through His Word on a daily basis. Even reading it for five or ten minutes a day led to wonderful conversations with God and chances to grow spiritually.

In 1987, Toronto pitcher, Don Gordon, invited Jerry to attend a Bible study conducted by Barry Banther, president of Trinity Bible College. That night, Jerry, at the age of 41, accepted Jesus. He knew that if he were to trust God with his life, he could experience the kind of joy and peace that the world just can't give. He asked the Lord to forgive him for the things he had done wrong and invited Jesus into his heart to totally direct his life.

These days, life is good for Jerry. He goes to his Source with any problems that arise. He treasures the Word, loves the Jays and lives by his motto: "Work like everything depends on you, pray like it all depends on God." —DRL

"Therefore humble yourselves under the mighty hand of God, that He may exalt you in due time, casting all your care upon Him, for He cares for you" (1 Peter 5:6,7).

‰ *100* ‰

Kelita

Because of Love

This five-time Juno nominee, known by music artists and audiences everywhere as simply "Kelita," has been recording for a total of 15 years now, sharing the stage with other celebrities. Joining her in the background vocals on one of her albums is well-known Canadian singer, Shania Twain. Yet despite reaping success and fame, Kelita decided to lay all that aside and fully pursue God.

Kelita has come a long way. As a child, she experienced the shame of abuse; as a teenager, her alcoholic father committed suicide and her Christian mother died of breast cancer. And if that wasn't enough for a young person to contend with, her brother overdosed on heroin and died a short while later.

During these difficult developmental years, life was filled with pain. And although Kelita gave her heart to the Lord in her teens, she walked away from Him and looked for love in all the wrong places.

Longing for a sense of security, she got married at a young age to a man who became her manager. Success came, but it left her empty. Nothing – not even drugs – could numb the pain and bring the happiness she so desperately sought. Then came a close brush with death which helped her to see the destructive road on which she was travelling. Miraculously, she walked away from a car wreck and took a second look at her life. "I knew that God had saved my life in that ditch," Kelita says with hindsight.

She knew many things in her life had to change, and one of them was to end her dysfunctional marriage. It took a lot of strength and resolve to get out of the abusive relationship. Soon after, a major contract with Nashville fell through. "I was left with nothing," she states. "Now, God could start healing me. I was ready."

During this time, Kelita received a powerful prophesy: "God is holding all your tears in the palm of His hand, and He is turning them into jewels that will be scattered over the nations to bring healing."

On her journey of healing, she met Gord Lemon, a bass player, music producer, and also a Christian. They married, but what should have been a "happily ever after" story, turned into another painful experience. However, this time, she had faith in God.

"*God gave us our future back.*"

Kelita

"During that most difficult period of time, when I wasn't certain whether our marriage would make it or not, I grew very close to God. I grew in my faith – faith in the future and faith in what I could not see and did not know. I really had faith that God would heal our marriage. He kept giving me more unconditional love for Gord. That was interesting to me, because in my first marriage, I did not have that feeling. I just wanted out.

"There were many months of uncertainty. But when everything came to a head, God began to change the desires of Gord's heart, and through that whole experience, God changed me too. There is a song, *Because of Love*, which is the title track of my new CD. God gave me His love for Gord, and He gave us our future back – together!"
—HS

❧ *Your Story* ❧

Mickey Robinson's testimony began this little book of stories and so perhaps it's appropriate that he should end it in his own words.

Mickey's Personal Message to You

A lot of people have misconceptions about God. Some of them think that if you live a good life, then good things will happen. But it's all based on the mercy of God – on the grace of God that was shown when He sent His only Son, Jesus Christ. And accepting it is not just fire insurance so that you won't go to hell. It's so you can have a life on earth that's different than what you've been living.

You could be going through a relationship problem, divorce, sickness or whatever. The thing you really need is a real relationship with God. It comes by saying, "God, I need You. I need Jesus Christ in my life."

Don't put it off. Just pray the following with me. It's simple:

> "*Dear Lord, I'm tired of trying to make it on my own. I'm sorry for my sins. Give me the grace to repent. Come into my life and change me. Reveal to me the purpose for which I was born. I want to live for You. I ask this in the strong and powerful Name of Jesus. And I ask the power of the Holy Spirit to touch me right now. Thank You, Lord. Amen.*"

If you prayed that prayer along with Mickey, please call one of the Crossroads prayer lines on the following page, or connect with us on the internet (www.crossroads.ca), and let us know. God bless you!

Crossroads Prayer Lines

A Crossroads prayer partner would love to pray with you for any special need you may be facing today. Simply call our prayer line nearest you:

Vancouver, BC	604-430-1212
Calgary, AB	403-284-4721
Edmonton, AB	780-944-0742
Regina, SK	306-781-8970
Winnipeg, MB	204-949-9414
Burlington, ON or USA	905-335-0100
Toronto, ON	416-929-1500
Montreal, QC	514-935-8814
Quebec City, QC	418-864-7448
Saint John, NB	506-674-2400
Halifax, NS	902-455-2600
St. John's, NF	709-738-2731

(Hearing impaired TDD # 905-335-6104)

A Special Invitation: **If you live in the Toronto/Burlington area and would like to join the ministry as a prayer partner, call the National Ministry Centre at: (905) 332-6400, ext. 2383**

Crossroads' Mission Statement

"The key objective of Crossroads Christian Communications Incorporated is to add to and bring unity to the body of Christ through direct and indirect evangelism; to enhance and augment the ministry of the local church; and to build understanding, credibility and attractiveness of life in Jesus Christ.

"This will be accomplished by the creative use of television and other media, together with other activities which respond to the mission conscience and needs of the constituency. The responsibility for outreach is to the world. Outside North America, C.C.C.I. responds only to the requests from organized and established Christian leadership. The role is as a catalyst to the development of indigenous and self-supporting ministry."

Accountability

Crossroads Christian Communications Inc. is federally chartered in both Canada and the United States as a charitable, non-profit organization. As such, it is funded wholly through free-will offerings. Crossroads is audited annually by Price Waterhouse Lybrand. Financial statements are available upon written request.

Crossroads receives the annual Seal of Financial Accountability from the Canadian Council of Christian Charities.

David & Norma-Jean

Lorna

Norm

Ann

Cal

Reynold & Kathy

The Crossroads Ministry

is made possible through the generous gifts of people like you who believe in Life-Changing Television. As many as 1.5 million individuals tune into the **100 Huntley Street** broadcast every week.

Crossroads' Emergency Response and Development Fund

This is a fund established out of compassion for people in areas of the world hit by disasters such as earthquakes, famine and war. Crossroads has sent millions of dollars in relief to the world's needy.

The Walk of Faith

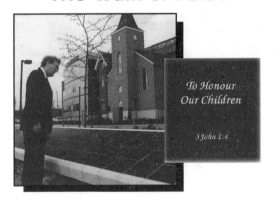

To Honour
Our Children

3 John 1:4

The Walk of Faith is a lovely walkway around the Crossroads Centre. Along the walkway are engraved granite stones which have been donated in honour or in memory of special people. Find out how you can join the Walk of Faith by calling **1-800-265-3100.**

Visit The Crossroads Centre

Here is a "to do" list of special Crossroads activities:

4 Join our live studio audience for *100 Huntley Street*
4 Tour the Crossroads Centre
4 Enjoy a special presentation in the Promise Theatre
4 Stay for lunch at the Towne Square Café
4 Browse in The Village Shoppe bookstore
4 Join our annual tour to the Holy Land

For further information and reservations,
call the Visitor Care department at:
(905) 332-6400, ext. 1281

**1295 North Service Road, P.O. Box 5100,
Burlington, Ontario, Canada, L7R 4M2
Phone: (905) 335-7100**

Visit the Crossroads internet homepage at:
www.crossroads.ca

Or send an e-mail message to: **huntley@crossroads.ca**